BE
BOLD

BE
BOLD

A Guide to
Unbreakable Confidence

ANNA GOLDSTEIN

ROCK
POINT
QUARTOKNOWS.COM
NEW YORK, NY

Inspiring | Educating | Creating | Entertaining

Brimming with creative inspiration, how-to projects, and useful information to enrich your everyday life, Quarto Knows is a favorite destination for those pursuing their interests and passions. Visit our site and dig deeper with our books into your area of interest: Quarto Creates, Quarto Cooks, Quarto Homes, Quarto Lives, Quarto Drives, Quarto Explores, Quarto Gifts, or Quarto Kids.

© 2021 Quarto Publishing Group USA Inc.

First published in 2021 by Rock Point,
an imprint of The Quarto Group
142 West 36th Street, 4th Floor
New York, NY 10018 USA
T (212) 779-4972 F (212) 779-6058
www.QuartoKnows.com

Rock Point titles are also available at discount for retail, wholesale, promotional, and bulk purchase. For details, contact the Special Sales Manager by email at specialsales@quarto.com or by mail at The Quarto Group, Attn: Special Sales Manager, 100 Cummings Center Suite 265D, Beverly, MA 01915, USA.

Library of Congress Cataloging-in-Publication Data

Names: Goldstein, Anna, author.
Title: Be bold: a guide to unbreakable confidence / Anna Goldstein.
Description: New York, NY: Rock Point, [2021] | Series: Live well |
    Summary: "Tap into your innate potential by taking practical steps to
    build your confidence with Be Bold."—Provided by publisher.
Identifiers: LCCN 2020046937 (print) | LCCN 2020046938 (ebook) | ISBN
    9781631067327 (hardcover) | ISBN 9780760369203 (ebook)
Subjects: LCSH: Self-confidence. | Self-realization.
Classification: LCC BF575.S39 G66 2021 (print) | LCC BF575.S39 (ebook) |
    DDC 158.1—dc23
LC record available at https://lccn.loc.gov/2020046937
LC ebook record available at https://lccn.loc.gov/2020046938

10 9 8 7 6 5 4 3 2 1

ISBN: 978-1-63106-732-7

Publisher: Rage Kindelsperger   Project Editor: Leeann Moreau
Creative Director: Laura Drew   Cover and Interior Design: Amy Sly
Managing Editor: Cara Donaldson

Printed in China

ACKNOWLEDGMENTS

Thank you to my husband, Jeff, for your love, encouragement, and unwavering belief in me. Thank you to my son, Evan, for being my teacher and guiding light.

I want to thank my mom and dad, Robin and Miles. You gave me the greatest gift of all, the gift of life. Ever since I was young, you have fostered my interests.

Thank you to my family—my brother Ari, Grandma Cynthia, Grandpa Rez, and all of my extended family.

A special thanks to Catherine Cusumano, Cindy Cornell, Sonya Furlong, and Caroline Zwickson for your support along the way.

A big shout out to Pat Verducci. I couldn't have done it without you.

Thank you to my friends who have been there for me during the ups and downs, and to my clients for unearthing my craft.

Lots of gratitude for my editor, Leeann Moreau, and publishing company, The Quarto Group.

I dedicate this book to all living beings. May everyone be happy and free from suffering.

You Got This

PAGE 08

1 The Voice in Your Head

PAGE 10

2 Befriend Your Fear

PAGE 30

3 Update Your Operating Belief System

PAGE 44

4 Connect with Your Intuition

PAGE 56

5 Become an Emotional Generator
PAGE 66

6 The Power of Visualization
PAGE 82

7 Blaze Your Trail
PAGE 96

8 Take Care of Yourself
PAGE 112

9 Nurture Your Confidence Seed
PAGE 128

RESOURCES   PAGE 141
INDEX   PAGE 142
ABOUT THE AUTHOR   PAGE 144

You Got This

We are taught that in order to be happy in life we have to succeed. And in order to be confident, we need success. But the opposite is true. In order to be successful in life, we must fail and get back up over and over again, each time acquiring new knowledge and growing our confidence. Each time we fall down and pick ourselves up, we build self-assurance.

Growing confidence means growing your belief that you can get through adversity, obstacles, and the everyday challenges of being human.

We build confidence through building ourselves. It comes from being with darkness and our weaknesses. Confidence doesn't manifest before you do something; it comes after you do things that make you scared. Taking action results in more confidence. Avoiding the hard stuff or shying away from what you want are speed bumps on your journey to being brave. Confidence comes from the hopeful act of knowing that *you are unbreakable*.

It's likely this book won't be one that you read in one sitting. Take time to process the information and integrate your learning. Consider working with a chapter a week to properly digest the material and incorporate it into your life. The most important thing is that this doesn't just become an intellectual exploration of confidence, but something you integrate into your life experiences. Go at your own pace.

In business and in life, people get stuck in their head, by overthinking, submitting to analysis paralysis, and letting fear stop them in their tracks. I've created a way to help people understand and take control of their thoughts and learn practical strategies so they can move forward and start living the life they really want.

This book is divided into two parts. The first is focused on creating awareness. Chapters 1 through 5 explore building your self-awareness as a method to connect with confidence. There is an aspect of self-awareness that includes discovering parts of ourselves that we don't know. And we must be open and willing to look at all these hidden places, deep inside. This requires us to sometimes admit we're wrong, enter the unknown, and connect with the bravery in our hearts that allows us to explore and create change in our lives.

The second part of the book, chapters 6 through 9, reveals methods and practical tools to build confidence. My goal is to guide you through a step-by-step process on your journey to confidence.

At the end of each chapter, I provide an exercise to support what you've learned. Acquiring new knowledge is necessary for growth, but applying what we learn creates even greater connections. Make sure you have a pen and paper or notebook and pencils to complete the exercises.

Every chapter closes out with a mantra. Mantras are a saying you repeat with intention and concentration about a personal aspect you wish to cultivate. Mantras help you create new pathways and thought patterns. Any thought that is repeated or tagged as important is stored and can become hardwired in your brain. Use the mantras to support you in taking confident actions. The intention is to provide you with insights and tools to grow the seed of confidence within you.

Confidence is something that you can learn to develop. It comes from the small things you repeatedly say and do. And if you shift just a single thought a day, things will look different.

Working together and finding an uplifting community can help you fully realize your potential. Join the bold community #beboldbook hashtag on social media.

The Voice in Your Head

1

"When you recognize that there is a voice in your head that pretends to be you and never stops speaking, *you are awakening* out of your unconscious identification with the stream of thinking. When you notice that voice, you realize that who you are is not the voice—the thinker—but *the one who is aware* of it."

—ECKHART TOLLE

I was twenty-five years old and living in a small studio apartment on the Upper East Side of Manhattan. As a girl who grew up in the suburbs of Maryland, I'd moved to New York City three years prior with big hopes and dreams for my future, but I was stumbling. I'd already had four different jobs, lived in three different apartments, and felt completely lost, alone, and isolated.

I was consumed by the voice in my head that told me all the things that were wrong with me, and I was worried about my future. Would I ever find my way in my career? Would I ever have a meaningful romantic partnership? How was I going to survive in this city financially? What if things didn't work out and I ended up poor, unhappy, and alone?

I obsessed over tracking my food; compulsively measured my belly, wrists, and chin, and constantly checked to see how much I weighed. I desperately wanted to be in a relationship to make me feel better and further distract me from my problems. But my biggest addiction was that I believed my negative thoughts.

I wished there was a switch in my head that I could turn off. But I couldn't. My nightly routine was to stare at the ceiling alone in the dark thinking I was seriously flawed. I was so consumed by the voice in my head that I spent several years like this— having trouble sleeping, not holding down a steady job, eating junk food, and drinking too much alcohol. I was so unhappy, my confidence plummeted.

But deep down, I knew there was more for me. I just wasn't sure what was in my way or how to access the strength within me. That little seed of believing there must be another way became my guiding light to seek answers and solutions to overcome my largest obstacle: my mind.

I knew I wasn't the only one struggling. In fact, I was the one many of my friends sought out to talk about their problems. Sometimes we would gab on the phone and complain about our lives for hours on end.

Maybe you too have been wondering how you can deal with the voice in your head that tells you, "You're not good enough, you're not qualified enough, you need more experience, something is wrong with you, you'll never be successful, you're too young (or old) . . ."

Is it possible to stop beating yourself up when you do something "wrong" or make a mistake? What would it be like if you didn't judge others, didn't care what other people thought about you, and instead went for the things you really wanted, even in the face of fear?

Maybe you feel like you just weren't born confident, that others have it all figured out, and because of your past experiences, you'll never be the person you want to be. Maybe you've done everything you thought would make you feel whole, and checked all the boxes, but you're still looking for a deeper sense of joy and fulfillment.

You know that you are meant for more. But how can you access your potential?

The Mind

The brain and mind are both important, and they are different. The brain is matter; it has a shape, size, and form. The mind is formless; you can't see or touch it. The mind is awareness itself. It's unlimited. And because of this, your potential is unlimited. When you learn to direct your attention and awareness, this acts as an invisible light that shines on your thoughts and feelings. It's an observer, there to witness information as it arises. You can use this understanding to change your brain and steer yourself toward confidence.

Over the last decade, neuroscience has been studying the effects of contemplative practices on the brain that produce psychological, physical, and spiritual benefits. This research proves that one of our biggest misperceptions is that we need something outside of ourselves to make ourselves happy. Rather, if we focus on the effects of our internal thoughts and emotions, we can find the happiness we seek.

The Brain and Negativity Bias

The primary purpose of the brain is survival. Since the brain is wired for efficiency and survival, we are equipped with a negativity bias, which is when our brain picks up negative information faster than positive information. Even if someone or a situation isn't a threat, our first reaction is to look for the threat. This was especially necessary in the infancy of humanity, when our brains were looking out for lions and other predators. The brains that always thought lions were lurking around the corner were the ones that survived. We try to avoid whatever hurt us in the past, so anything that resembles that threat triggers a reaction, as if we were facing an actual "lion." We are constantly looking out for threats to our survival.

Research shows that most of our daily thoughts are focused on something negative and can be quite repetitive. Because of that negativity, we tend to ruminate on what went wrong rather than what went right. By overthinking things, we can get caught up in what we lack instead of focusing on what we have. When we worry about the future, we completely miss the chance to enjoy the present. These inclinations to make ourselves suffer are hardwired into our brains.

If you experience negative thoughts, you're not alone! Instead of blaming yourself (or your mind) for having negative thoughts, try to understand that this is a natural part of your brain. Instead of fighting it, learn to work with it. If we acknowledge that our brains tend to exaggerate threats and overlook opportunities, we can adapt our responses appropriately.

Negativity bias can lead us to get caught up in rumination, overthinking, worrying, and negative-thinking loops. This is because it's easy to take a piece of information and create a whole storyline in your head about what's wrong or could go wrong, and your body responds as if it were true, feeding this storyline even more. Without further investigation, these cycles keep churning.

Have you ever had the experience of getting super-positive feedback from a boss—they tell you how well you did on communicating with the customer and following up, and what a pleasure it is to work with you—but then, they share a tiny observation that you need to work on speaking up in meetings more? What do you focus on? The fact that your boss thinks you don't speak up enough in meetings. Your mind will gravitate towards the piece of feedback it perceived as "negative." This is the negativity bias at work. Even though it's operating to protect you, it's a reaction that's not always or completely accurate. The negativity bias takes a piece of information and exaggerates it rather than looking at the whole picture.

If you're curious about whether your fearful reaction to something is in response to an actual or a perceived threat, you will discover that a threat, like a mirage, often appears as though it's real, but it's not. There are many great benefits to being able to distinguish between a perceived threat and an actual threat.

Self-Perception

The negativity bias also affects how we perceive ourselves. We tend to focus more on our negative qualities than on our greatness. We believe the thoughts we think about ourselves around being stuck, insecure, or fearful. We might have tried to make changes in our lives and failed and we begin to believe that this is "just the way we are."

Here's the thing: you are attached to the way you currently view yourself because it's the "self" that you know. When you start challenging or questioning what you "know" about yourself, it can feel unsafe. Since your brain is wired for safety, and you feel that your sense of self is being threatened, you can get defensive, reactive, and guarded. You react by protecting the identity you built and when someone says or does something that contradicts those ideas, your natural impulse is toward fight or flight.

Have you ever had the experience where you thought you couldn't do something, but then did it? You later realized your perception was incorrect. When you can change your perception of yourself, things change. This is the power you have.

If you are used to identifying with yourself as insecure, lacking in confidence, or incapable, then that's how you show up in the world. In a world that is constantly telling you "you aren't enough" and "you need more," I'm here to tell you that you already have what you need. You are born with wisdom, and it's likely that you got bogged down by so much outside noise that somewhere along the way you lost connection with your innate confidence.

If you keep listening to what everyone around you says, and continually seek external validation, it is likely that when you finally achieve what you thought would give you confidence, you'll be disappointed. You'll realize validation might feel good for a moment, but true confidence can never come from something outside of you. Believing in yourself comes from your thoughts and feelings.

I've learned how to turn down all the outside noise and turn up the volume of my true self, and that's what I want to teach you. Part of being confident isn't about having it all figured out but knowing that while you are figuring it out you can still be a confident work in progress.

Nothing stays the same—your bank account will go up and down, relationships will come together and fall apart, your weight will fluctuate, and so on. You can learn to face challenges and your confidence will be unaffected because you don't attach your worth to those things. Unconditional confidence comes from feeling grounded in the truth of knowing you are a good person and, because you have a good heart, you are enough just as you are.

If you want to change your life, you must change the "negative" story you tell yourself—the inner dialogue about what's wrong with you, where you have failed, why you can't. Let's examine how these negative storylines are created, and how we can work with them, rather than try to escape them.

Self-Conscious to Self-Aware

Part of the growth process involves being able to recognize the negativity bias as the voice of the ego. The ego is fearful, judgmental, self-obsessed, defensive, and rarely rooted in the present. In the quest to protect your sense of self, your ego can lead you to playing small in life.

The ego is the voice in your head urging caution, and it does this to protect you and look out for danger. While it is necessary to know you are physically safe, in reality, listening to this voice can lead to being overcautious due to fear. Your ego equates certainty with safety and uncertainty with a lack of safety. And when it urges undue caution, it can hold you back from stepping into the unknown.

Any threat to our identity is perceived as a threat to our survival by our ego. If you want to expand your life you need to recognize your ego's attraction to what's certain, familiar, habitual, and comfortable. Develop your awareness to be a witness to the voice in your head rather than beholden to it.

Understanding the voice of your ego is essential to becoming self-aware, and is the key to transformation. Distinctly different from self-consciousness, when someone is self-aware, they know themselves intimately. They observe their thoughts and are able to experience insecurities without feeling insecure. A self-aware person lets go of feelings of unrest easily and is open to learning.

Everyone has insecurities, but how you manage them makes all the difference. Commanding them isn't about pretending they aren't there, but rather facing them head-on. Since humans are blessed with consciousness, we have an incredible ability to grow, expand, and transform our consciousness from ego to awareness. If you face it through awareness, the voice gets smaller, becomes fainter, and eventually has less power over you.

FACETS OF THE EGO

Imagine your ego voice almost like a separate entity with its own agenda to basically make you feel bad in service of what it deems "protection." Your ego voice often uses words like "I" and "me" in a limiting way. It uses phrases such as, "I'm not good enough," "Something's wrong with me," and "Why can't I get ahead?"

Embedded in these phrases is a global sense of "me" being defective. The ego has trapped you into thinking that you are the most important person in the room (or even on the planet). Your entire perspective revolves around you. Yes, you are important, but let's face it—not everything is about you. Sometimes your boss is having a bad day and it isn't about you. The ego thinks it's the most important thing in the world (even when it's thinking it's not enough!); every mistake has a spotlight on it; every "bad" thing you did or ate seems like the worst thing in the world.

When I'm working with a client, I typically ask, "Who do you think about all day?" They reply, "Myself." Understanding this can help free them from the burden of worrying what other people think about them because they are reminded that everyone else is thinking about themselves, too.

Next time you're unhappy, uncover the storyline. A story is a cluster of negative thoughts that creates a narrative that *feels* true. It's helpful to investigate it to discern whether it *is* true.

Are you focused on you and what you don't have? What you did wrong? How often are you concerned with "What about me?!" Constant self-obsession is the root of suffering.

You might be thinking, "Not me, I think about others all the time." I invite you to look more closely at how you think about others. Do you think about others as they pertain to you? For example, you might think about your boss . . . but whose boss is it? You might think about your partner . . . but whose partner is it? You might think about your family . . . but whose family is it? In all of these scenarios, you are the central figure.

Everyone on some level believes they are not good enough. Every single person. No matter how rich, famous, or beautiful, everyone experiences feeling not good enough. When you know that everyone feels this at one time or another, it doesn't need to be something that controls you, that you automatically believe.

Normally, when your ego feeds you a thought, you would immediately accept it as truth. When you think your thoughts are who you are, and you automatically believe things like "I am anxious," you feed into the narrative and then further become an anxious person to support the identity "I am anxious."

However, avoid judging yourself or making yourself feel wrong for having negative thoughts. This will only create more negative thoughts! Your ego isn't bad. It's part of being human. You don't need to push negative thoughts away. Now is the time to develop an unconditional friendship with your ego. Get to know it so well that you become the creator of your life rather than letting it run the show. Underneath the ego armor, the fear, and the defense mechanisms, is a softness. Contrary to what we normally believe, gentleness and vulnerability are where we discover our true power.

HERE ARE SOME OTHER BASIC WAYS YOUR EGO MIGHT SHOW UP:

COMPARES: Focuses on what's lacking after observing others. *"Look what she/he has that I don't have . . ."*

DEFENDS: Stubbornly keeping opinions regardless of the facts. *"I'm right, you're wrong . . ."*

FEARS: Potentially crippling and unwarranted anxiety and fear of the unknown. *"I might get rejected, so I'm not going to try . . ."*

ATTACKS: Lashing out through anger, disappointment, or other emotion that the ego thinks it needs to defend itself from. *"I am a stupid idiot . . ." "That person is a jerk . . ."*

COMPLAINS: Discontent where the only action is unproductive criticism. *"Things should be different . . ."*

FEELS EMBARRASSMENT: Projecting personal shame on the world's perception of you. *"Other people think I'm stupid . . ."*

JUDGES: Always looking for what's good or bad, right or wrong. *"How could they?"*

A FALSE SENSE OF SELF: Tries to please your ego instead of your true self (heart, intuition) by over- or under-inflating. *"I'm the smartest person . . ." "I'm not good enough . . ."*

SEPARATES: Ignoring that we are all connected. *"I would never . . ."*

FEELS INADEQUACY: Always wanting or needing more and never content. *"I need . . ."*

PROJECTS INTO THE FUTURE OR THE PAST: Letting your mind essentially live in another time rather than being present. *"What if . . . ?" "Why did that happen?"*

CREATES A STORY: A negative narrative unfolds that may or may not be true. For example, your ego might tell you things. *"I'm bad at relationships. The relationships I've been in never seem to work out. Something must be wrong with me. Why can't I figure this out?"*

SHIFT FROM THINKER TO OBSERVER

The first step in gaining awareness is to notice your thoughts. Normally, we don't even pay attention to the fact that we're thinking; we just accept whatever track is playing in our head as background noise. Or we might even be afraid to hear what our thoughts are saying because we think that our thoughts are true. So, when that voice says "I am a bad person," we run from this voice and get into habits that stem from low self-esteem. In that moment, we limit our sense of self.

Begin to notice that thinking is happening all the time—and recognize that these thoughts arise and come and go. Treat them as thoughts, without believing they are true. Watch your thoughts come and go like clouds, coasting through a clear blue sky.

Some people are so consumed by thinking the voice in their head is who they are, that they've lost the ability to live beyond their current reality. They can't listen to anyone or anything else. Have you ever asked someone a question and they answer what they think you said and not what you actually said? This is how you can recognize when others are so consumed by the voice in their heads that they are not present.

You must apply the practice of catching yourself in repetitive storylines and shift from thinker to observer. This is not easy.

Being an observer of your thoughts is not about forcing thoughts to go away, making thoughts bad, or making yourself wrong for having negative thoughts. Being the observer is about having a gentle light of awareness that takes stock of your stream of consciousness. When you observe a negative thought, you have the ability to say something like:

- "I never realized how often I put myself down."

- "Isn't that interesting how often I feel insecure or fearful."

- "I notice I get angry when I feel like I've been treated unfairly."

The act of noticing is a practice you will continue to repeat over and over again.

This doesn't mean that once you have this awareness you do nothing. With awareness, you can take action, communicate your needs more clearly, and move forward with a sense of confidence because you aren't following the limited story in your head.

The greatest freedom you will experience is not in something external: getting the perfect job, having a certain amount of money in the bank, or having a great body. The greatest freedom is internal—it is the power to understand your mind.

Increase Your Awareness

"To see one's predicament clearly is a
FiRST STeP toward going beyond it."

—ECKHART TOLLE

Once you become aware of this egoic monologue in your head, you can interrupt these patterns and create new thought pathways. It's common to have an unrealistic expectation that all of a sudden you can completely transform. You will fall into old thought patterns, but it's important to be able to recognize, "Oops, I'm in an old thought pattern." Eventually, you will create new ones.

One night when I couldn't sleep and my thoughts were racing, I picked up the book *The Seat of the Soul* by Gary Zukav. I had tried to read this book on many occasions, but it didn't make sense to me. Until this one night, when I started reading and every word on the page resonated. I learned that the root of my unhappiness and behavior was that I was in survival mode and the pursuit of external power was making me feel powerless. Zukav stressed that a new kind of power, authentic power, could reshape the world. That if I aligned my personality with my soul, I could create meaning, purpose, creativity, health, joy, and love. This was the beginning of my awakening and learning to become a witness to my fear-based thoughts.

I spent the next several years reading books and practicing yoga, meditation, and more. I don't claim to be awakened, but I am on the path. My definition of "awakened" means I am no longer consumed by the voice in my head. And because of this, my confidence has continued to increase.

Without judgment and with gentle recognition, each time your mind wanders or gets lost in worry, fear, or doubt, recognize it. Watch the language you use in your head and when you interact with others.

* How do you speak to yourself?

* How do you describe yourself when you interact with others?

The more you practice observing your thoughts, the more authentic power and confidence you will have.

My life isn't perfect. There are still nights when I stare at the ceiling, overthinking; there are days when I feel uneasy, and times when I doubt myself—but they are fleeting. I don't have everything all figured out. But I can be confident while I am still learning and growing.

Confidence isn't about being perfect. It's about understanding the truth of who you are. It's about using your inner creativity, resourcefulness, bravery, curiosity, passion, and heart. It's about trusting yourself even when you don't have it all figured out. It's not about what you achieve, but who you become along the way.

You can see that your confidence is growing when things that used to spin you into a negative thought pattern, or knock you down emotionally, no longer do—or if they do, they don't knock you out for such a long time. When you fall down, or have bad days, you recover quickly.

Watch Your Language!

Another doorway to becoming more aware of your thoughts is to watch your language. The words you use and the way you describe yourself, events, and experiences greatly influence how you feel and the actions you take. Notice how it feels in your body to say something like "I'm stupid" versus "I'm smart." Can you notice how each of these thoughts brings with it a completely different quality of energy? It's likely that the more encouraging thought is lighter, whereas the condemning thought is heavier.

Words carry a vibration. Each thought you think makes an impact on your cells, and your body responds accordingly. Many people think it's funny to put themselves down, to use sarcasm when they interact with others or without really understanding the power of words. Imagine two children starting out in life: one grows up with a parent who is constantly criticizing them and the other grows up with a parent who is supportive in their language. Think about the impact. The words you use sculpt your brain and emotional landscape.

I'm not talking about taking a "negative" thought and simply replacing it with a "positive" thought (although that can be helpful at times). I'm inviting you to be aware and search for

"Your mind is a *GARDEN*. Your thoughts are the *SEEDS*. The harvest can either be flowers or weeds."

—WILLIAM WORDSWORTH

what is really true. Ask yourself, "Is this thinking helpful?" or "What else could be true?"

IKEA partnered with the agency Memac Ogilvy Dubai to do an experiment and show the effects of bullying on plants. It brought its experiment to a local school, GEMS Wellington Academy in Dubai, so students could witness the results in person and even take part in the experiment themselves. "The live experiment involved IKEA taking two of its very own plants and installing them at the school. Both plants were treated strictly the same," a press release said. The plants were provided with the same amount of sunlight and water, but one plant was played recordings on a loop that included positive phrases like, "Seeing you blossom makes me happy," and the other heard negative words like, "You look rotten." The results, after 30 days, were that the plant that listened to positive affirmations remained green and lively, but the plant that was "bullied" turned brown and began to rot.

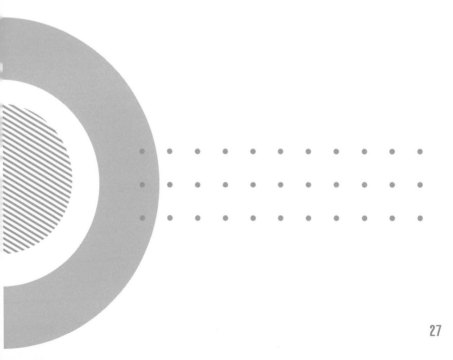

GET TO KNOW YOUR EGO

What's a repetitive negative thought you have, or a negative story you tell yourself? This thought or story might start with something like:

* I'm not good enough at . . .

* I'm too . . .

* Something is wrong with me . . .

* If I had ___ then I would be able to . . .

* I need more . . .

* I'll never . . .

Close your eyes and repeat the negative thought or story in your head intentionally. Then ask yourself the following questions:

* Where in your body do you feel this thought? Is it coming from your head? (Often the voice of our ego feels like it's coming from above our shoulders.)

* What is the pace of the thought? Is it fast or slow?

* What's the volume of the thought? Is it loud or quiet?

* What feelings arise when you have these thoughts? Do they feel tight or expansive?

* What type of imagery do these thoughts bring to mind? Are these pictures limiting or expansive?

* When you are consumed by this voice, what does your behavior look like? What kinds of actions do you take?

Now that you are aware of how your specific ego voice sounds, you can start your confidence journey.

I AM ENOUGH

JUST AS I AM

BeFRIeND
YouR FeAR
2

"Usually we think that *BRAVe PeoPLe* have no fear. The truth is that they are intimate with fear."

—PEMA CHÖDRÖN

The number one thing that stops us from being truly confident is fear. But it's how you respond to fear that can allow you to grow. The idea is to not try to remove fear but to welcome it and turn toward it. It's important not to think fear is "bad" or "wrong," that you shouldn't be fearful, or that you should be naturally courageous. Safety is a basic need, and we want to learn how to feel safe enough to bet on ourselves, go after our dreams, take risks, and leap into the unknown. What makes confident people different is that they feel fear and take action anyway. They don't wait until fear is absent to take action. Learning to act in spite of your fear is essential for building confidence.

We all experience fear. On some level, we all recognize our vulnerability. We are afraid of loss, pain, and getting hurt. Everyone has their own path and lessons to learn. No matter their title or what they have accomplished, there is no escaping the human experience of fear. Recognizing that fear is a human emotion stops you from putting others on pedestals and therefore making yourself smaller in comparison.

Fear has a useful purpose: to protect you. But you need to differentiate between fear that warns you because of a truly dangerous situation, and the fear of doing something new and expansive that the brain can register rather than helpful for growth. Fear can propel you to take positive action because you are afraid of a negative consequence.

The Confidence Myth

We are taught that to become confident we need to toughen up so that we appear strong. We think being strong and confident means being stoic, unafraid, and consistently brave. Someone might be very social and friendly and appear to be loved in all situations. However, deep down, this might be a façade to cover insecurities about being liked and loved.

The myth tells us that confidence is "fearless." And we judge ourselves as lacking because we have fears. We feel that vulnerability is a weakness. But if we are too rigid and we let life experiences harden our hearts, we become limited and closed off. The idea is to be able to be courageous enough to not hide behind a façade and to be open to whatever arises. The way to confidence is to continuously befriend ourselves—no matter what happens—in a genuine and loving way. Loving yourself unconditionally means being able to be with yourself, even when you feel weak or afraid. This is how confidence is built.

Real confidence means we can sit with our vulnerability, be kind and compassionate, and not harden ourselves into something we're not. When we can be soft, we can really lean into the depth of our hearts and help others do the same.

Confidence Through Failure

Most of us grew up learning that "failure is bad." We have the general understanding that we should do well in school and not get "bad" grades. Our culture doesn't teach us or normalize how to deal with setbacks, sadness, or disappointment, so we grow up internalizing it. When we internalize failure, we let it dictate our behavior. We might say, for example, "I screwed that up, I should never try that again!"

Failure can come with some great benefits. Through failure, you recognize your strength (I survived!). Through failure, you recognize resilience (I am resilient!). Applying what you learn through failure encourages personal and professional growth. Moving through life with a sense of resilience and the ability to bounce back after failure inspires confidence for bigger challenges. Anyone who has ever achieved their dreams failed at them first.

Why do you fear failure? You fear failure because you don't think you can handle losing love, connection, money, or your reputation. It's often not the actual failure itself that creates the fear, but the anticipation of experiencing some kind of loss. This is essentially what it means to worry: to anticipate future suffering. We think, "What if something goes wrong? How will I survive?"

The greatest risk is not taking risk. It is through failure that we learn the greatest lessons life can teach us. Every letdown is feedback that can lead you toward achievement.

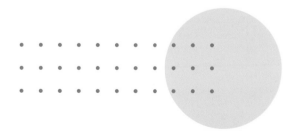

The Law of Familiarity

The lobster's shell is hard and can't expand. As it grows, the shell gets tighter and tighter, and the lobster gets more and more uncomfortable because it is stuck in that constricting shell. Eventually, the lobster gets so uncomfortable that it decides to do something about it. It goes somewhere safe, sheds its protective shell, and grows a new shell that fits its new form better. The lobster repeats this multiple times as it grows bigger and bigger. Each time, it's the discomfort that encourages the lobster to grow a new shell. Without this discomfort, it would stay small and within the limits of its comfort zone.

This example applies to humans as well. As you grow up, you build an identity of who you are to create a sense of belonging. Identity is necessary for your development and to create a sense of who you are in the world. However, sometimes these identities become limiting in adulthood and no longer serve us. It's at this point that growth happens: when we need to dissolve our current shell in order to grow into a new one.

The set-point theory of happiness suggests that our level of subjective well-being is determined primarily by heredity and by personality traits ingrained in us early in life. In other words, we all have a fairly stable "set" level of happiness—some people experience a lot of happiness, others a low amount, and most of us, somewhere in between. No matter what happens to us,

> "You will either STEP FORWARD into growth or back into safety."
>
> —ABRAHAM MASLOW

Risk and Reward

Self-made billionaire Sara Blakely, founder of Spanx, an intimate apparel company, says her father's focus on failure actually helped her become the success she is today. Every night, her father would ask her what they had failed at that day. She began to associate failure as not trying rather than trying and not succeeding. And she came to believe that it's worse to live with regret than to fail. This gave her the courage to start a fashion brand with no fashion experience. She says, "Don't be intimidated by what you don't know. That can be your greatest strength and ensure you do things differently from everyone else."

whether we're up or down, we generally tend to drift back to our original "set point." So even though you might desire a "healthy" body, you might drift back to poor eating habits. As you begin to train for a race, you might backslide into Big Macs and onion rings. We take two steps forward and then take three steps backward into "safety" and "familiarity." This usually happens when we experience fear. We all have comfort "set points"—the points at which our mind starts to convince us why we should stay where we are.

What's familiar has already been proven to be safe. Any time you do something new, there is uncertainty, which can give rise to stress, anxiety, and a feeling of lack of control. Recognize these emotions as natural reactions. Develop your ability to differentiate between something that is actually harmful and unsafe, and something that is just new and feels uncomfortable. You can remain safe and grow through the discomfort. Practice moving toward new sensations and experiences (if it's not dangerous to do so!).

ACKNOWLEDGE FEAR

There are two primary motivations behind behavior: to avoid pain and to seek pleasure. Obviously, it's natural to want to avoid pain. Because we are wired for survival, we reject pain and habitually react in ways that keep us safe or confined to our "protective shell." Here's the thing, though: growth is uncomfortable, and it often involves some pain. If you are always looking to avoid pain, you also prevent growth.

Short-term discomfort can lead to long-term pleasure. For example, you might want to watch Netflix instead of exercising. But if you are willing to endure the short-term pain of exercising, it will lead to long-term benefits. We've all had the experience of suffering though a painful event that we later grew from. For instance, withdrawing from a toxic relationship can be agonizing, but this withdrawal allows us to see why and how we got into the relationship in the first place, and this insight allows us to embark on positive relationships in the future.

In order to grow, we must learn to change our relationship with pain. Just like we can't expect to build muscle without the pain of pushing ourselves beyond what's comfortable, growth involves some discomfort. Everyone has a growth edge: it's that place where you bump up against the edge of your comfort zone. You know that stepping over the edge is scary but will ultimately lead to more freedom.

Train yourself to move through pain and discomfort. Can you look at discomfort as a playground for learning? Could you be lighthearted with yourself, not take yourself so seriously? Could you be like a child learning to walk, falling down, maybe crying for a moment, but getting back up to continue walking? You have the ability to change your relationship with pain, and instead of seeing it as something that is "bad," see it as something that enables "growth."

Just like you and I, fear wants to be acknowledged. So, say hello. "Hi, fear! I see you. I feel you. But you are *not* me." Once you acknowledge fear, you are no longer consumed by the "trance" of fear and it loses its power over you.

Here are common fears that we experience.

COMMON FEARS

* Failure
* Not being good enough
* Abandonment
* Loss (money, love, etc.)
* Rejection

* Being alone
* What others think
* Being judged
* Getting hurt
* Suffering

Working with Your Fear

It's time to normalize feeling and experiencing discomfort and fear. Do things that scare you. Instead of letting fear and discomfort make you suffer, learn how to use pain as a building block to strength. When building muscle in your body, the muscle grows when it is introduced to higher levels of resistance or weight. This process is known as muscle hypertrophy. Muscle hypertrophy occurs when the fibers of the muscles sustain damage or injury. The body repairs damaged fibers by fusing them, which increases the mass and size of the muscles. Think of your tolerance for fear and discomfort in these terms as you build strength and confidence.

Learn to work with the energy of fear. You can do this by using the following mindful techniques. Mindfulness helps you get out of your head and into the present moment. When feeling fear, use these strategies to ground yourself:

1. **Name five things in your physical environment. For example, a chair, a table, a computer, a water bottle, a pair of shoes.**

2. **Do box breathing. Close your eyes and breathe in for four seconds, hold your breath for four seconds, breathe out for four seconds, and hold for four seconds. Repeat four times, or until you feel calm.**

You can work with fear in small ways. Maybe you speak up at work when you feel afraid, or you sign up for a race, or make a connection with someone you admire, or post something vulnerable on Instagram.

CRAFT DESIRES BIGGER THAN YOUR FEAR

Working as a coach, I notice that often when I ask the question "What do you want?" people don't know. Or they regurgitate some version of what they were taught to want and think this is truly their own desire. Conforming is so ingrained that most people haven't even thought that it might apply to them.

There is a natural desire to belong, to live life within the lines and make all aspects of the way we live look good to gain the approval of others. From a very young age we are taught to make our parents and teachers proud. And if we don't listen, we get in trouble. So, we learn to follow along and behave. We learn to make others happy, and then we carry those same behaviors into adulthood.

Take a minute and think about it. What do you *really* want?

Choose Your Focus

Find something you fear more than what's stopping you. For example, maybe you're afraid of being in a relationship but you're more afraid of being alone. Maybe you're afraid of rejection but you're more afraid of living a life you're not happy with.

In my early twenties, I struggled to find the "right" career path. I was trying to do what I thought I should do and get a "9-to-5" job. But I had a calling deep within my heart to make an impact and have my own business. After being fired from several jobs, I became more afraid of working for someone else than working for myself. Placing my livelihood in another company's hands was scarier than going independent. Was I afraid of going out on my own without having much of a net? Yes. Did I let it stop me? No.

Focus is power. Where you focus your attention can make all the difference in the actions you decide to take. To progress toward what you really want, focus on the benefits. Ask yourself, "What can I gain? What if it works out?"

Here are some Things to Remember about Fear

* Fear is a natural reaction to new situations.

* Fear snaps you out of autopilot, and you become more awake and alert.

* Working with fear allows you to live life to its fullest.

* Failure and loss can help you build strength and resilience.

* Every time you do something you didn't think you could, you expand what you believe you're capable of.

* When you move through a fear, you develop confidence.

FEAR MAPPING

ANSWER THE FOLLOWING QUESTIONS. BE TOTALLY HONEST WITH YOURSELF.

* What do I really want?

* What is keeping me from achieving what I want?

* What am I afraid of?

* Look back, where does it come from?

* Does the reward outweigh the risk?

* Look forward, where does it keep you from going?

* What are the negative consequences if I don't go after what I want?

* What are the benefits of going after what I want?

FAILURE IS A stepping-stone TO SUCCESS.

It is safe for me to grow.

3

Update Your Belief Operating System

"You must *Feel Deep* in your gut that not only has this belief cost you pain in the past, but it's costing you in the present and ultimately, can only bring you pain in the *FuTuRe*. Then you must associate tremendous pleasure to the idea of adopting a new, *eMPoWeRiNG BeLieF*."

—TONY ROBBINS

A belief is a thought you have repeated so much that you accept it as truth—whether it is true or not. Over time, you accumulate beliefs that form your identity in the world. This is necessary for our sense of belonging and understanding. These beliefs have become part of how we filter and navigate our actions. However, just because you come to certain conclusions about yourself based on your experiences, doesn't mean that they are absolutely true.

Just like your computer has an operating system that needs to be upgraded, your belief system sometimes needs a reboot. This is because most of us are walking around with old, outdated operating systems, ones that were installed in our childhood, adolescence, and early adulthood. One of the ways to build confidence is to continually update your belief operating system, rather than allowing yourself to be permanently tied to the ideas you created from interpretations of your past.

Reality vs. Our Interpretations

Since we are always looking to make sense of the world around us in order to survive, we assign meaning to our experiences. Events and experiences happen in our life, and from them, we create beliefs. We humans attach meaning and make up a story to fit most everything we see, hear, and experience. However, reality is subjective, and our version of "reality" is filtered through our belief operating system.

Nothing inherently has meaning until you assign it meaning. When you understand that *you* create what things mean, you become empowered to choose. Is the breakup of a relationship "the end?" Or is it "the beginning?" Is life happening *to* you or is life happening *for* you? Every day you are creating meaning around the events in your life. Most of the time when you're upset about a situation, if you examine what you made an incident mean, you will quickly realize that what's making you feel upset is not the actual situation but the meaning you've assigned to it.

Examine Your Belief System

Growing up, we often internalize someone else's behavior as "something to do with us" when it has little or nothing to do with us. For example, as a child, you couldn't see that Mom was going through a difficult time at work. You saw Mom come home from work and yell at you if you spilled something. That led you to believe, "I made a mistake. Mistakes are bad. I am bad." But really, this was false. Mom's frustration was about work, not you.

We also do this in adulthood—someone treats us poorly and we think, "I did something wrong," instead of "They're having a bad day." This doesn't mean that we shouldn't take responsibility for our actions, but instead of taking things personally all the time, we need to look at the whole picture.

Several years ago, I coached a women in her mid-twenties who was in a toxic relationship. She was a health enthusiast and her boyfriend was an alcoholic. It was clear she was having a hard time leaving the relationship. When we began to peel back beliefs she had about relationships, she explained that her parents got divorced when she was eight years old. She remembers when they told her that they no longer were going to be married, she felt an incredible pain. In that moment, she decided, "I will never leave someone. It's too hurtful." When she realized she had created a belief about herself ("I will never leave someone"), she was able to update her belief to what was actually true for her. "If I am in an unhealthy relationship, it's okay to leave." She left the relationship and a few months later met a man who is now her husband.

Ego drives us from a very young age to personalize perceptions of situations and circumstances that are often not the whole picture. Additionally, beliefs and perceptions can be handed down for generations or built in from societal and cultural beliefs. They can be learned from family, friends, teachers, or experiences, and stem from our need to belong. Sometimes your beliefs are phrases that were repeated to you by the world around you, such as "go to college," "work hard," "get a good job," "get married," and "have kids."

Many beliefs can seem helpful to give us a sense of direction, but we need to examine whether they truly work for our lives. It is in our best interest to identify and call out the societal messages that limit us. For example, women in the past were taught to believe that they should want a handsome prince, straight out of Disney. Princess stories demand that women have to look a certain way and have a certain body type, and that men are meant to save them while they take care of the house, keep their mouths shut, and follow along. Oh, and they *never* sweat.

You might notice that you have been influenced by messages like these in subtle ways, especially if you're feeling bad for not being married by a certain age, are stuck in a good job but really want your own business, or something else that goes against what you've been taught. This influence can manifest itself through practiced excuses for why you can't do something, or in believing that you're "too much," or the nagging feeling that you shouldn't (or can't) do things alone. Once you recognize the beliefs that limit you, you can break free of them.

Supporting Evidence

The mind will almost always look for proof that it's right. Instead of searching for the truth, it will seek out evidence to support the way it already thinks. For example, if you believe guys are jerks, this becomes a filter through which all you see is men who are jerks. There might be plenty of kind men, but your mind will cancel them out and carefully point out the jerks to prove your belief. Remember how we talked about negativity bias? This phenomenon is called confirmation bias.

The reticular activating system (RAS), which is located at the base of the brain, acts as a filter to all the "data" around us. This includes sounds, tastes, colors, images, and any other sensory input. Your brain can only process so much at a time. So, your RAS flags only things that it thinks are important to you. How does it know what is important? By what you focus on most. Therefore, if you are focused on what's wrong in your life, what will you continue to see?

I often take clients through an exercise where I have them look for everything in their room that is orange. Then I have them close their eyes and I say, "Tell me everything that is blue in your room." And since they were looking for orange and not blue, they can only tell me up to three things they know are blue in their room. Then they open their eyes and they see many things that are blue. The blue things in the room were always there but they weren't looking for them, so they didn't see them.

Your mind is like an internet search engine. What you place in your search box dictates the information you get back. This is why it's important to focus on what you want to create. Remember the hang glider inventor? That person didn't focus on the impossibility of jumping off a building and flying, but how it *could* happen, and then came up with a design that made it possible.

Be mindful of where you put your focus, because your RAS will show you proof and the more proof, you see, the more you strengthen your belief that this focus is true.

● ● ● ● ● ● ● ● ● ● ● ●

Perception is Power

A young teacher was working in a high school in New York. When he got the job, he was told he would be working with high-achieving students, so he took that mind-set with him to class on the first day. The class was chaos. When one student threw a chair out the window, he went to the principal and the principal asked, "Was anyone hurt?" The teacher said no. The principal said to go back to the classroom, that's not a problem.

Throughout the chaos, the teacher kept in mind that his students were high achievers, so he used methods to teach them as if they were high achievers. During the middle of the school year, someone from the administration came to him, wanting to recognize him as a great teacher. He would not accept the recognition. There were too many behavior problems in his classroom, he said, and he did not feel comfortable accepting an award. But by the end of the year, the principal insisted on giving him an award for excellent teaching because the scores of his students had gone up tremendously. The principal then said, "We want to recognize the work you have done, considering you were working with underachieving students."

What?! Clearly, he'd misheard what the principal said about the students when he was hired.

He received so many letters from students thanking him for believing in them, for teaching them at a high level, and many said they would not have gone to college if it hadn't been for this teacher.

Believe in Possibility

Did you know that what's possible is a matter of opinion? Yeah, sure, there are some fundamental scientific laws, such as gravity. For example, it's impossible for a human to just jump off a building and fly. However, someone took into consideration the scientific laws of gravity and aerodynamics, and the belief that it is possible to jump off a building, and built a hang glider.

Maybe you are fully capable of doing that thing you've been doubting you can do.

Could you look at the things you have deemed impossible and see them in a completely different way? Could you believe in possibility?

This story illustrates the power of perception. How this teacher perceived his students affected the way he taught them. How you perceive yourself dictates how you take action. If you perceive yourself as confident, how might this change your behavior out in the world? You are more capable than you think.

Develop a flexible mind-set. Perception originates in you and only through working on yourself can you change the way you view the world. There is power in questioning what you believe and exploring new beliefs. When you are aware of your old operating system, you can update it.

Confidence is in You Already

A common belief about confidence is that confident people have to be loud, extroverted, attractive, smart, strong, successful, wealthy, and have it all together. But these qualities don't guarantee confidence. Some of these people are the most insecure, especially because their happiness and confidence are so dependent upon external conditions.

But confidence isn't outside of you. It's not something you need to chase or acquire. Confidence isn't in pretty, or skinny, or money, or your career. Truly unbreakable confidence can be found in quietness, introversion, any body type, being okay not having it all together, vulnerability, and caring.

Confidence comes from carving your own path and knowing that your path doesn't have to look like anyone else's. Confidence is knowing that you can change and grow. Confidence is connecting with the truth of who you are—unlimited potential. There is no limit to your greatness.

We are all unique individuals. There is no one mold for what confidence looks like. Personally, I find confidence in being my most authentic self and trusting in my basic goodness. I can rely on my good heart and intentions as a source of stability. This allows me to be brave and face challenges, knowing that I'm doing my best.

UPDATING YOUR BELIEF OPERATING SYSTEM

A limiting belief is something that holds you back from your goals. For example, you could think that you're not pretty enough, or that money only causes trouble.

An expanding belief is something that creates opportunities and confidence and supports a desirable future. This belief can be something like you are already beautiful, or money can empower you to achieve what you want.

Fold a piece of paper in half and write Old Limiting Beliefs on one side and New Expanding Beliefs on the other. Re-frame each negative belief into an expanding belief to start changing the way you think.

RECREATE THE PAST

To free ourselves from the past, we have to confront it. Use the following space to allow vulnerability into your being and lean into your feelings. Once you feel your emotions, you will be able to have better control of them.

See if there are some negative stories that you tell yourself that can be rewritten now that time has passed.

What happened in the past? (painful events and experiences)

What did I make those painful events mean? (beliefs, conclusions, your interpretation)

What actually happened? (state the reality; use only facts and avoid feelings or your interpretations of what happened)

What can I see now that I couldn't see when the event happened?

What's my new belief? (about past events and experiences)

What opportunities are available to me now?

BE
BOLD
BE
YOU

I can change my beliefs.

Connect with Your Intuition

4

"Your time is limited, so don't waste it living someone else's life. Don't be *TRAPPED BY DOGMA*—which is living with the results of other people's thinking. Don't let the noise of others' opinions drown out your own inner voice. And most important, have the *COURAGE TO FOLLOW* your heart and intuition. They somehow already know what you truly want to become."

—STEVE JOBS

We mostly pay attention to the world through the five senses of touch, sight, hearing, smell, and taste, and yet, this is limiting. Yes, you can see light with your eyes, hear a car horn with your ears, smell and taste a bite of buttery corn, and feel the prick of a cactus if you touch it. But you also have senses that go beyond this. Multisensory perception is the ability to sense beyond how you normally perceive yourself and the physical world. A multisensory perception might appear as a hunch, gut feeling, nudge, or just "knowing." This wisdom is not based on a fleeting thought or emotion, but is embedded in your body and is sometimes called your intuition or instinct. According to the Oxford dictionary, intuition is the ability to understand or know something immediately, without conscious reasoning.

I believe we are born with innate intuitive wisdom but somewhere along the way, something happened and you stopped trusting yourself. Confident people have learned to listen to their intuition and act on it. Listening to your intuition is a skill you can learn, even after years of discounting it. Clients often say,

"I hear my intuition, but I'm not following it." That's because the logical or rational, egoic part of our brain will try to shut down the intuitive voice.

For example, your intuitive voice says,
"I want to start a business."

Your rational, egoic voice says,
"I have no business experience."

Your intuition isn't always rational. It's there to guide you to your highest potential. Your intuition may come to you through a quiet voice, an image, a gut reaction, or an inner hunch. It rarely screams at you like your ego does. But to access your intuition, you must first believe that you have this inner knowing, even if the belief is slight.

When I lived in New York City, in my mid-to-late twenties, I lived in seven different apartments. I kept renting rooms from people because I couldn't afford a rental apartment by myself. Finally, after living in an apartment for only six months, my roommate told me I needed to go. I was so upset that I left the apartment and went to the gym. I remember standing in the locker room looking at myself in the mirror, tears welling up in my eyes, and I thought, "My life isn't working out. I should just move home and live with my parents until I can figure out my life." And then, when I really looked into my own eyes, the tears stopped. I was able to recognize in that moment that these thoughts were making me upset. I was able to recognize I was not the voice in my head.

So, I asked myself, "Anna, what do you want?" And I heard my intuition say, "I want my own business. I want to live in New

York and get my own apartment." Then I realized that I could make this dream a reality and I granted myself permission to do so. Next, I asked myself, "What do I need to do to create this for myself?" Determined, I went home and started crunching numbers and making budgets to see how I could live in New York on my own.

Two months later, I found my own apartment. Three months later, I went on a blind date with a man who would become my husband. Five months later, I established my own business. If I had listened to the voice in my head and made the decision to move home based on what my head was telling me, my life would look very different than it does today. And not in a good way!

When you aren't confident, it's common to ask other people, "What do you think?" I want to encourage you to start tuning in to what *you* think—what you want, what you feel, and what your intuition says.

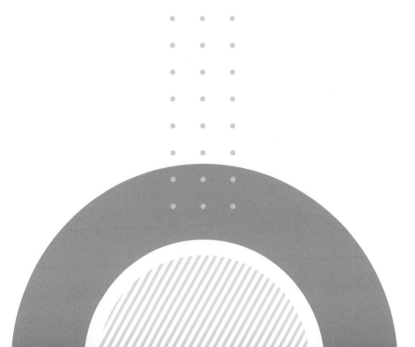

Give Your Intuition a Megaphone

How do you learn to recognize and listen to your intuition? These methods can help:

1. **SLOW DOWN.** I call this the purpose pause. Check in and notice. When faced with a decision, ask yourself, "What does my intuition say?" Continue to ask yourself this question. Listen for the answer and then follow its lead.

2. **REDUCE STIMULATION.** Overwhelming stimuli can also make it difficult to see the decision in front of us with clarity. Urbanization, large crowds, noise, television, social media, and the explosive growth of information can become louder than your intuition. Decrease stimulation overload so that you can get in tune with yourself.

3. **SELF-CARE.** What activities make you feel good and in flow? Do baths make you feel centered? Do walks help you feel calm? Fold them into your routine.

4. **MEDITATION.** If your mind is too busy, it can be hard to hear your intuition. Meditation is the practice of learning to notice thoughts, let go of the mental chatter, direct your attention, and create a sense of calm. Meditation strengthens concentration and helps you learn to cultivate a deeper sense of body awareness. By training your mind to recognize when you are caught in thought loops, and how to come back to your focal point, meditation helps you get centered and calm.

More on Meditation

Meditation often looks like the following: Sit in a relaxed way with your back straight and your chin parallel to the floor. Gently close your eyes.

To ground yourself and focus your mind, spend a few minutes concentrating on the sensations of your breath as it comes in and out of your nostrils.

Then begin a body scan. Start with the top of your head and spend a minute or two really focusing on all of the sensations, then slowly move your attention all the way down your body to your toes. What do you notice? Where do you feel tightness? If you feel nothing, that's okay. With practice, you will start to pick up more subtle sensations.

Each time you notice distraction creeping in, bring that watchful mind back to the breath. This guidance should be gentle and without judgment. Even if you just simply notice how busy your brain is, bring your attention back to the task at hand. At the very beginning of your meditation practice, the process should focus on noticing how scattered your attention is and how difficult it is to focus. There is a misconception that when you meditate you should empty your mind completely, but that is not true—the key is to learn to observe your thoughts and increase awareness. When you notice how distracted you are, you are meditating, because the moment you recognize you are not present, you become present.

A review study at Johns Hopkins University looked at the relationship between mindfulness meditation and its ability to reduce symptoms of depression, anxiety, and pain. Researcher Madhav Goyal and his team found that the effect size of meditation was moderate, at 0.3. If this sounds low, keep in mind that the effect size for antidepressants is also 0.3, which makes the effect of meditation sound pretty good. Meditation is, after all, an active form of brain training. "A lot of people have this idea that meditation means sitting down and doing nothing," says Goyal. "But that's not true. Meditation is an active training of the mind to increase awareness, and different meditation programs approach this in different ways."

I use guided meditations on YouTube and I attend classes at the Kadampa Meditation Center in Boston. There are many types of meditation, and I encourage you to investigate local and digital resources to develop your own meditation practice. It's a great way to connect with yourself.

Starting your practice may not be easy, especially if you have never done it before (which is true for anything new you do). If you have never played the piano before, you wouldn't sit down and expect to be able to play a piece by Beethoven. That's why meditation is called a *practice*. Every time you meditate, you strengthen your ability to manage your mind, which is a key component in connecting with your intuition and feeling happier and more confident in yourself.

LISTEN TO YOUR INSTINCTS

Turn down the volume of your ego and turn up the volume of your intuition. Let the whispers be heard. Strengthen this connection with yourself. You can practice in small ways, such as decisions about what clothes to wear, what to have for lunch, and so on. Practice making decisions from your intuition.

When I began to practice this, my first challenge was shopping for a winter coat. I was in a boutique trying on two coats. One coat had faux fur on the hood and went a few inches above my knees. The other coat was more expensive, had no fur on the hood, and went about an inch above my knees. My mind was rationalizing price and style and I was having trouble making a decision. Once I asked my intuition, though, the choice was clear and simple. The more expensive coat felt better and, ultimately, I liked it more. I bought the coat knowing I was making the right decision.

I try giving my intuition a megaphone, by listening to and acting on it, whenever I can.

CONNECT WITH YOUR INTUITIVE COMPASS

Think of a time when you knew something just because it felt right. Maybe it was a time where you moved, or left a job, or made a change in your relationships. Go back to that moment when you made that decision and think about what physical sensations you felt in your body.

* ★ What was the pace of hearing this intuitive voice? Fast or slow?

* ★ What was its volume? Loud or quiet?

* ★ Where in your body did you feel this knowing?

* ★ What was the feeling that arose when you connected with your intuition? Tight or expansive?

When you look to yourself for guidance, you receive it. When you start leaning on your intuition more, you may mistake the limiting voice in your head or your belief operating system for true guidance, but keep trying and listening. Gradually, you'll come to know what your intuition is telling you. Serena Williams doesn't get her first serve in every time, even though she's been practicing it for over thirty years. But just like Serena continues to practice her serve, continue to practice listening to and using your intuition. Confidence comes from trusting your intuition. With practice, you can train yourself to incorporate more intuitive actions and thoughts into your daily life.

I PAY
ATTENTION
AND TRUST
MY
INTUITIVE
NUDGES.

5

Become an Emotional Generator

> "No one can make you *feel inferior* without your *consent*."

—ELEANOR ROOSEVELT

We all understand that in order to become physically fit we need to eat well, sleep well, and engage in physical exercise. But we often don't consider that emotional strength is also something we can train for. You can become emotionally fit by raising your emotional intelligence and becoming an emotional generator.

Emotional intelligence is defined as a person's ability to identify emotions (in both themselves and others), recognize the powerful effects of those emotions, and use that information to inform and guide behavior. An emotional generator is someone who uses their emotional intelligence to understand how they currently feel, determine how they want to feel, and figure out how to generate this desired emotion. Confidence is an emotional state. It's the by-product of using emotional intelligence to acknowledge your feelings and tap into empowered states that propel you to action.

It's not that confident people don't experience "negative" emotions, they just choose to relate to them differently. When you are emotionally fit, you don't let other people or external events dictate how you feel. Studies have shown that people with high emotional intelligence perform at higher levels at work, have more harmonious relationships, and are happier overall.

Emotions are Energy in Motion

Developing emotional intelligence is learning to be the watcher and see the wave pass when discomfort arises or use the energy underneath the wave to direct it toward something good. It's learning to use everything in your life to lean in and listen, rather than turn and run.

None of us is exempt from distressing emotions—feelings of fear, vulnerability, and despair. These emotions are part of the human experience. Sometimes we are so consumed by our own feelings of insecurity or fear that we forget that our boss, partner, parent, and grocery store clerk also have these same feelings.

Growing and expanding involves experiencing these "negative" emotions. I use the word "negative" in quotes because certain feelings are uncomfortable, but that does not mean they are necessarily bad. For the purpose of this explanation, I will use emotions that don't feel good as "negative."

In fact, every emotion is useful if we use the information inherent in it to become more curious and aware of our feelings. It's not easy to deal with uncomfortable emotions, but learning to face them head-on is the key to sustainable happiness and unbreakable confidence. If we don't deal with difficult emotions, we can become reactive and short-tempered, hurt others, and limit ourselves. Although it might feel like discomfort is coming from the outside world, feelings originate inside you. Since they are coming from within, with awareness, you can learn to work with the energy of emotions in your body. Labeling your emotions will help you become responsible for your emotional state and interact with your feelings in productive ways.

When you're feeling an intense emotional energy, P.A.U.S.E. Use this to investigate your feelings and to create a life you love.

P: Perception. Notice what you're thinking. Write down your thoughts.

A: Attune. Feel what you are feeling. Allow emotions and sensations to be there.

U: Understand. Ask yourself questions. What is the situation? What am I longing for?

S: See. Look for alternative views. What else is possible?

E: Energy. Embody confident energy. What would my confident self do?

Label Your Emotions

When you label your emotions by giving them a name, you can adequately process these feelings, instead of suppressing them and releasing them in unproductive ways. The goal is to allow the emotions to move through you. Stopping to identify the emotion helps create distance between yourself and the experience of the emotion. This is a helpful tool when you are learning how to respond to challenges and adversity.

Below is a list of emotions that you might have experienced and are able to label for yourself. All of them are fear-based, but it's helpful to specifically name the type of fearful emotion. Take note of how you typically react when you experience the following emotions.

. . . .

Shame

Shame involves believing that you are "not good enough" and feeling a sense of wrongdoing. Shame makes you want to hide the part of yourself that feels wrong. Through courage and vulnerability, you can heal shame by labeling it, seeing it for what it is, and realizing you are okay and that this emotion is shared by all human beings. Understanding that you are not alone can help you become more empathetic to others.

Doubt

Simply by acknowledging this emotion, you can begin to work through it so it doesn't hold you hostage. Doubt can lead you to investigate your truth.

Resistance

It's natural for human beings to resist change. Resistance appears as a feeling of thickness and difficulty. We know we have to do something, but we "don't want to." We come up with justifiable reasons to prove why we shouldn't do this thing. However, to get what we want, we often have to do things we don't want to do. Resistance is sneaky, using "logic" to feed itself. If you're feeling hesitant, overcoming resistance can start with the smallest action toward your goal. Look for the lowest barrier to entry. For example, if you're resisting working out, put on your workout clothes.

Frustration
If things aren't going the way you expect, or if you feel as though you are being treated unfairly, or are caught up in how you think things should be, it's easy to default to feelings of frustration. Frustration feels like a low, angry simmer. However, it can be fuel to move you in a new direction because it is often giving you important information about what you need to change.

Anxiety
Anxiety is a feeling of worry, nervousness, or unease. Often this is the result of a misguided use of the imagination, which projects all the things that could go wrong. There's a lot of "what if" thinking with anxiety and obsessing about horrible outcomes. You are focused not on the present, but on the future. Anxiety can inform you about where you are out of alignment.

Impatience
Too many people set big goals and quit or give up when it doesn't meet their time-bound expectations. They want it now, and they are in a hurry, which sabotages their objectives. Change is a process, and because setbacks are inevitable, it's necessary to cultivate a sense of patience. Great things require time, and ultimately patience is what will create lasting results.

Sadness

No one wants to feel sad. Sadness can manifest as feeling sorry for ourselves or dropping into victim mode. We blame others and feel powerless. We turn away and don't want to look. But sadness can also move us toward compassion and healing. When we take responsibility and embrace sadness head-on, it can show us what we really care about.

Perfectionism

Perfectionism is getting so caught up in the details that we procrastinate and rarely move the needle in our life or business forward. We become perfectionistic when we believe we need to be perfect in order to receive love and attention. When we know that we already are love, we have the freedom to choose progress over being "perfect."

Labeling a difficult emotion, giving it a name, and recognizing it will allow you to take the reins back, even if it's only for a brief moment. When you shine light onto emotions you typically want to ignore, deny, or hide from, you gain authentic power and emotional resilience. You gain confidence that you can handle your emotions. You begin the process of moving from emotional reactivity to choosing an emotional response. True power comes from having a choice.

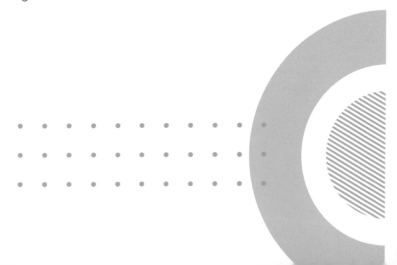

The Foundation of Emotional Fitness

The foundation for any healthy relationship, including the one with yourself, is trust. When you have built a foundation of trust, even when you make a mistake or hear criticism, it doesn't rock your boat. Maybe for a brief moment, you default to your "negative" comfort zone, but then you bounce back rather quickly. This builds optimism.

According to Dr. Aparna Iyer, psychiatrist and assistant professor at the University of Texas Southwestern Medical Center, "Optimists do acknowledge negative events, but they are more likely to avoid blaming themselves for the bad outcome, inclined to view the situation as a temporary one and likely to expect further positive events in the future."

There is a saying that "every problem has a solution." There is always a light at the end of the tunnel. How do we know that there is a light at the end of the tunnel? Because no feeling is ever permanent. It's comforting to remember the saying "This too shall pass." Sometimes we can't see this right away because we are in the intensity of the emotion. We default to our negative comfort zone. But if we trust that things will get better, and take action based on that trust, we build optimism. You can train yourself to be solution focused.

Why We Need Emotional Fitness

The most powerful force in the world is human emotion. This invisible force is what moves us to action. It allows us to connect, create community, and make change. The ability to consciously choose your emotions can change your life and those of the people around you. You might have heard the phrase "Happiness is a choice." While that may be partially true, the whole truth of it is that people who are happy do not seek happiness from others, or by purchasing cars or houses. Happiness is an inside game.

Just as happiness is an inside game, so is confidence. Confidence is relying on your inner resourcefulness rather than external resources. Instead of focusing your attention on the possessions or circumstances that are absent from your life, you can make your own confidence and happiness by shifting your attention to what you have and what you can do.

Sometimes our emotional "home base"—a place we default to—might be "negative" and familiar. For example, do you typically feel frustrated? Sad? Disappointed? Discouraged? Where is your emotional home base? Learning to recognize when you are stuck in your emotional home base and then directing your attention to what you want to create is an invaluable self-coaching tool. It's possible to stay in touch with your emotions but not be overwhelmed by them.

Instead of going to your default emotional home base, you can consciously choose and lean into how you want to feel. Here's how.

1. When life throws you curveballs, how do you want to respond?

2. Create your new emotional home base. How do you want to feel?

3. Bring those feelings to life in your body. Really take them in and tap into your sensory awareness. Where in your body do you feel this emotion?

4. Anchor that feeling so that in the midst of stressful situations you are able to access your new emotional home base. An anchor is a trigger or stimulus that helps retrieve a desired emotional state. For example, recall a time that you felt "I've got this!" and tap your foot three times. You can then use tapping your foot three times to recall the thought and feeling "I've got this!" Having an anchor helps you shift from your default "negative" emotion to a more empowered one.

The difference between living by default and living by design is choosing how you want to show up to life every day. And then, moment-by-moment, making that choice again-and-again.

Transform Adversity into Opportunity

Everyone has had an experience where they wanted a situation to work out a certain way, and it didn't. Hopefully, later, you were able to look back and think, "I gained so much from that experience." If you view problems as growth opportunities, you'll become far more adept at handling them quickly, efficiently, and with less stress. You can actually gain a lot from adversity, if you look for the gifts.

Your current life is perfectly designed for growth. I believe everything that happens to us helps us become more conscious. The more conscious you are, the more confidence you will experience.

Sometimes you don't know how something is working *for* you at the time, but later it becomes clear. Sometimes, the adversities you faced in childhood can create your superpower as an adult. The following anecdotes describe people who transformed their childhood adversity into opportunity.

Sarah was adopted and felt like she never fit into her family. This was a constant struggle for her growing up and led her to question her sense of belonging. She knew she stood out as a tall blonde with her short brunette parents. She wanted to look like them, and not like herself. But guess what? Now her superpower is capturing her clients' one-of-a-kind personality and style and helping to brand them and reveal their unique qualities. She aims to help her clients stand out—miles (and millions) above the competition. This superpower (the ability to make others stand out) directly relates to the shame, sadness, and anxiety she felt for being "different" as a child. She now can see that her childhood "disadvantage" is her greatest gift as an adult.

Richard Branson, founder of Virgin Records and Virgin Atlantic, has dyslexia. He was also a pretty bad student and did poorly in school and on standardized tests. He dropped out of school at age sixteen, saying his dyslexia was "treated as a handicap" and his teachers thought he was lazy and dumb. He couldn't keep up or fit in. Instead of giving up, he used the power of his unique perspective of the world to drive him to success. One of the strengths people with dyslexia often have is a vivid imagination. Thomas Edison, Henry Ford, and Steve Jobs were all dyslexic. While most of the business world is caught up in facts, figures, and details, Branson was able to think big, keep his message simple, and innovate using his strength to conceptualize.

As children, we are sensitive, constantly adapting to situations and our environment. Many people blame their past for why they aren't where they want to be, but what if they could use the skills they developed because of the adversity to propel themselves forward?

Create Your Emotional Engine

A car engine is fueled by burning either diesel or petrol in a combustion chamber. The axle turns the wheels and makes the car move forward. The purpose of a gasoline car engine is to convert gasoline into motion so that your car can move. Consider that fueling yourself with the energy of faith, courage, inner peace, joy, passion, and love can move you forward. These are your emotional fuel. They never were outside of you, nor do you need to achieve anything to get them. They are always inside you and you can practice using them by giving them extra attention.

Hardship and adversity can allow you to become more compassionate, creative, and determined. You can use these past experiences to create a better future. Pain can be a great motivator if you learn to use it to justify why you are capable. Making it through difficulties is how you learn strength and emotional resilience. Know that because of the adversity you faced, you can get through hard times now and in your future. Make what you've been through the reason why you are capable of taking on challenges.

* Maybe dealing with a difficult parent helped you become more curious about human behavior.

* Maybe being bullied in school helped you demand respect in adulthood.

* Maybe having an alcoholic parent taught you ways to be resilient.

* Maybe your father wasn't around a lot growing up, so you decided you want a partner who is involved.

* Maybe your parents getting divorced helped you realize the type of partnership you want.

* Maybe watching others make bad choices guided you to be more methodical in your own choices.

Contemporary meditation master Sayadaw U Tejaniya, author of *Awareness Alone Is Not Enough*, puts it this way: "When you experience good mind states, actively remember them. Remind yourself that you are experiencing a good mind state, that good mind states are possible, that this is how a good mind state feels. In this way you reinforce the understanding of the good states you experience."

Make a decision to live in an emotionally empowered state. Seek out empowered emotions, notice them, and let them fuel you. When you master emotion, you gain power to master your life. Every time you put your attention on an empowered emotional state, you strengthen the emotions that make you feel fully alive.

The exercises at the end of this chapter are some ways to seek out and reinforce these emotions.

DO CONFIDENCE REPS

Contrary to what we would like to believe, cultivating an attitude of confidence isn't easy. It requires conscious effort to identify our emotions and practice the emotions we want to feel.

Think of a moment in your life when you felt really confident.

* What made you feel confident?

* What are you celebrating in your life?

* What are you excited and passionate about?

* What song makes you feel pumped up?

Here are some ways you can practice feeling confident:

* Recall a time when you felt confident and use that feeling as an anchor.

* Practice walking with confidence.

* Speak up when you normally stay quiet.

* Do things that scare you.

AN OBSTACLE IS THE OPPORTUNITY TO GROW.

ADVERSITY GIVES ME STRENGTH.

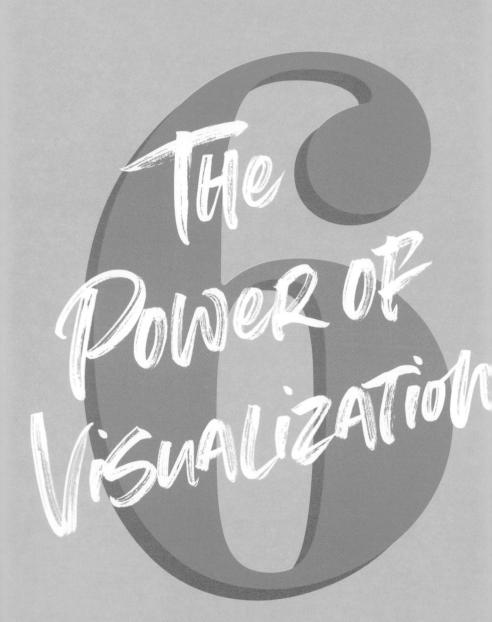

6

THE POWER OF VISUALIZATION

> "*IMAGINATION* is more important than *KNOWLEDGE*."

—ALBERT EINSTEIN

Some of the most extraordinary things we use today started as wild ideas. The plane you fly in, the pen you use to write with, the phone that keeps you in touch with your friends . . . none of these existed until someone imagined them.

It's common to believe that having the "right" qualifications, experience, and knowledge can help you succeed. But what gives the most successful people in the world an edge is they know how to use their imagination to direct their attention, emotion, and focus to what they want to create. Having a compelling vision gives you energy, inspiration, and direction.

Visualization is one of the most powerful tools to help you break through mental barriers. Too often we place emphasis on acquiring knowledge instead of the limitless benefits of creative imagination. Using your imagination can improve your problem-solving skills and boost your self-confidence. Picturing how you want to be is a skill you can always use to help you navigate new territory and achieve new accomplishments.

How Visualization Works

The human brain thinks in terms of visuals and pictures. If you close your eyes and think of a "pink elephant," you will probably see an image of a pink elephant. Visualization is a proven process. Athletes, entrepreneurs, coaches, and leaders use visualization as a tool to help them achieve their goals.

When you visualize doing something, you stimulate the same brain regions as when you actually perform that same action. A well-known study, popularized by Ellen Rogin and Lisa Kueng in their book, *Picture Your Prosperity*, speaks to the power of visualization in the world of elite athletes. Russian scientists in this study compared the training schedules of four groups of Olympic athletes.

* Group 1 had 100 percent physical training.

* Group 2 had 75 percent physical training with 25 percent mental training.

* Group 3 had 50 percent physical training with 50 percent mental training.

* Group 4 had 25 percent physical training with 75 percent mental training.

The results showed that Group 4—with 75 percent of their time devoted to mental training—performed the best. By creating strong mental images, athletes primed their bodies to what they imagined into reality.

Visualization is a proven step to success because picturing something vividly—and with a lot of detail—forces the brain to make these goals seem closer to reality. In sports, it can also help smooth over anxieties and other distractions so that athletes can better focus on the task at hand.

When you have already visualized a scenario, the real thing will be more familiar and feasible. It will be as if you've done it before, because inside your mind, you have.

Mental Rehearsal

I first learned about the power of visualization when I was a senior in high school. I was eighteen and had been playing competitive tennis for the past nine years. I was about to compete in the Maryland State Tennis Championship tournament. I was seeded number 2, which meant I was supposed to come in second place. But I knew, deep down, that I could win.

My mom found an ad in the paper about a sports psychologist and sent me to her. I met with the psychologist for a few weeks before the competition. And while I had physically practiced a lot during that time, in our sessions, the psychologist helped me embed in my mind the fact that I had practiced, and this reaffirmed my confidence in my strokes. I pictured myself winning the tournament. I saw myself walking with confidence, feeling what it would feel like to perform at my best, and be the Maryland State Champion.

The day of the championship match the weather was perfect—sunny with a slight breeze. I felt different walking on to the court. I quickly won the first game. In between points, I was walking with confidence, just like I had imagined. That championship match was the best tennis I ever played. I was what athletes call "in the zone." I became the Maryland State Champion, just like I had visualized.

From this experience, I clearly saw how my mental preparation impacted my performance. Having a clear mental visualization strengthens neural networks and unconsciously shapes your behavior so that you reach your goal.

You Can Create Yourself

Mental imagery isn't just for people who play competitive sports. Visualization can be used to prepare for something as simple as having a difficult conversation (imagining yourself calm and relaxed) to something as life-changing as finding a romantic partner or starting a new career. Professional musicians commonly rehearse difficult parts of a musical passage by performing the piece of music in their minds. Mental rehearsal activates the same motor, auditory, and emotional circuits as playing the actual instrument.

Lady Gaga says that she created Gaga before she became Gaga. Stefani Germanotta was born in Manhattan, New York, in 1986, and by the age of four, she was learning piano. She studied people she admired who came before her. Her first persona/alter ego was called Candy Warhol. At 14 she started playing in jazz clubs. In college, her performances were fairly conventional and during her sophomore year, she dropped out to pursue her music career full time.

Quickly, she discovered that audiences in bars and nightclubs were much less attentive than college art students. As she recalls, "There was this one night where I had had a couple of drinks. I had new material, and I had on this amazing outfit. So, I sat down, cleared my throat, and waited for everyone to go quiet. It was a bunch of frat kids from the West Village, and I couldn't get them to shut up. I didn't want to start singing while they were talking, so I got undressed. There I was sitting at the piano in my underwear. So, they shut up. That's when I made a real decision about the kind of pop artist that I wanted to be."

Germanotta moved her sets to burlesque clubs. She worked on her musical skills, but she also worked on her persona.

Ultimately, she combined burlesque, performance art, and music to create Lady Gaga.

But she didn't just visualize who she wanted to be. She began to embody this person. She worked hard and took the necessary steps to bring her vision to reality. There were obstacles, detours, and challenges along the way, but she stayed focused on her vision for herself.

"Life isn't about *FINDING YOURSELF*. Life is about *CREATING YOURSELF*."

—GEORGE BERNARD SHAW

Be Open to Detours

Expect that things won't go as planned or how you visualized them. Yes, my Maryland tennis victory unspooled just as I had imagined, but most of the goals I've achieved didn't unfold exactly like my original vision. There were qualities and characteristics of the actual events that were similar to my imagined version, but not exactly. Sometimes when you are too attached to expecting things to happen a certain way, it narrows your perspective and you miss opportunities to create your vision through different avenues.

In 2000, professional triathlete Siri Lindley was preparing for the Olympic trials in Sydney, Australia. She set a goal that every single day, she was going to visualize the perfect race, executing every moment beautifully and crossing the finish line as the winner, making the U.S. Olympic team. Every night for 365 days, she went through this visualization process of the perfect race from start to finish.

On the day of the Olympic trials, the gun went off, she dove into the water, and within 15 seconds, she got kicked in the face by another swimmer and lost the front pack. This was not in her visualization, and she didn't know how to respond because she hadn't prepared for it. She completely choked. The race began to feel hard, people were passing her, and she failed to qualify for the trials.

Thereafter, she made changes in her training and visualizations. She decided that if she were in a crap position, she would just put her head down, go as hard as she could, and see how close she could get to the front. A year later, in 2001, she became the ITU Triathlon World Champion and qualified for the Olympics.

Lindley choking in the Olympic trials in 2000 helped her understand that in life, yes, you want to be able to visualize things going well and achieving your ultimate goal. But you also need to anticipate things going wrong and build up the confidence in your visualization to see something going wrong and handling it with grace and composure.

The incredible lesson here is that when you visualize— whether it's for a race, a meeting, a date, or whatever it is—yes, you need to visualize things going great, but you also want to visualize things going wrong and see yourself overcoming these challenges.

When I was soul searching in my mid-twenties, I started tapping into visualization again. It had worked in my tennis career, so I thought, "Why not apply it to my life and career?" I felt completely lost. At that time, the common perception of a "good job" was one that involved going into an office, sitting at a desk all day, wearing "real pants," catering to your boss, and waiting for payday. Frequently, I invite clients to think about their career based on the lifestyle they want to create. This is often very different from the "good job" that they learned was the only way to succeed. What if they want to wake up, meditate, and work from home or have a flexible schedule? What if they want to wear yoga pants all day and make a ton of money while having their dog curled up on their lap?

Instead of trying to visualize a "good job," I began visualizing my desires. I knew I didn't want to sit at a desk all day in "real pants," and I used the things I knew I *didn't* want to clarify the characteristics of what I *did* want. My "ideal day" began to come

The Power Pose

Stand with your feet apart, your hands on your hips, and your chin tilted upward. These small tweaks to your body language can produce psychological and behavioral improvements in your mind-set.

Practice:

* Standing with confidence

* Walking with confidence

* Talking with confidence

You can do this when no one else is around, in the privacy of your own home, walking down the street, or even in the car. And you can practice it when you are with your coworkers, at a networking event, on a date, or with friends.

into focus. I wanted to have my own business, have the freedom and flexibility to go to yoga when I chose, and make a positive impact in the lives of others. I visualized myself becoming a life coach, having my own business, and wearing yoga pants most of the day.

At the time, I was nowhere close to achieving my vision. I was working a 9-to-5 job doing internet marketing and I had zero experience as a life coach. So, I looked up an actual life coach I found on the internet and reached out to her. I told her why I was passionate about becoming a life coach and asked if she would meet me for coffee.

During our coffee chat, I asked her questions about what she did and how she did it. I shared with her my passion to become a life coach and told her my story about how working on my mental game with a sports psychologist impacted me. I courageously asked if I could work for her. A couple of weeks later, she gave me the opportunity to work for her as an assistant/mentee. I quit my job and enrolled in an NYU Coaching Certification Program. I was so excited! I thought, "This is my dream job!"

But as I began working for her, things started to unravel. I wasn't getting as much work as I thought she had promised. She told me I was doing reports "wrong" and began getting frustrated with me. My confidence and excitement plummeted. After so many jobs not working out, I wanted for this one to work so badly!

Several months later, it was clear we weren't a good fit to work together, and I needed to go back to the drawing board and get a new job. I started working at Equinox fitness as a sales representative. I loved fitness, but I had no idea how to sell. I took their sales training course and worked on my side-hustle life coaching business. After five months of working at Equinox, I had made some new friends and one of them set me up with my husband. If I hadn't taken that job, I probably wouldn't have met him. I also learned sales skills that helped me in my business. So, as you can see, the detours led me to learn and develop a clearer understanding of what I wanted, and the specific actions I took made them (and more!) happen.

Action Leads to Clarity

See yourself moving through challenges and obstacles with confidence. How do you respond when you get "rejected"? What do you do when something doesn't go as planned?

Keep taking action and don't let detours stop you. Expect detours. Welcome them. Growth isn't about speed, distance, or perfection, but moving steadily in the right direction.

Let go of your attachment to a certain time line. Let go of *when* it will happen and *how* it will happen. Keep your attention on *what* you want and *why* you want it.

Action leads to clarity. As you take these steps, your vision for yourself will get clearer. If you don't have a clear vision yet, just keep taking action toward the things that make you feel the emotions you want to feel. Each step will move you forward.

Imperfect action is better than no action. Focus on progress over perfection. You might need to pivot or adjust your route, but don't give up on your vision.

LETTER TO A FRIEND

One of the best ways to clarify your vision is to write a letter to a specific friend telling them what your life looks like. Date this letter two years from today. Write it in the present tense. Transport yourself two years into the future and tell your friend where you are, what you have or do, what you've accomplished, and so on. What is different about your life, career, relationships, or business? How has this desired outcome affected other aspects of your life? Are you thinking differently about things?

Fill the letter with descriptive details that will assist you in anchoring this vision to reality. When you visualize, it's important to make your vision as clear and specific as possible. Engage your five senses to make this visualization so real that you can feel it in your body. This may seem ridiculous at first, since we can't predict the future, but this letter will supercharge your direction. Have fun with it!

* If you want, you can use the following prompts to get you started . . .

* What does your ideal day look like?

* How do you feel (what are the emotions) in your body?

* How do you dress?

* How do you handle rejection, setbacks, and detours?

I CREATE MY OWN REALITY.

BLAZE
YOUR TRAIL

"Do not go where the *PATH MAY LEAD*, go instead where there is no path and *LEAVE A TRAIL*."

—RALPH WALDO EMERSON

Your vision defines who you want to be and your aspirations. One way to think about your vision is the idea of reaching for the stars. The act of moving upward is what makes our day-to-day life meaningful.

Think of your vision as a guidepost and not some future destination. You want to unhinge from the idea that you are not enough and not get caught up in the rat race to reach the proverbial mountain of success. Your vision's purpose is to inspire you to act in accordance with your potential. It's not to show you where you are falling short, how limited you are, that you're "not there yet," or "how far you have to go." You're not meant to withhold confidence and fulfillment until you've "arrived" at some specific destination.

If you are waiting to feel confident until you've achieved your vision, you will likely miss out on much of your life. It's a cliché to say "enjoy the journey," but why do people say that? The process is what needs to be fulfilling. You want your vision to be cultivated by enjoying the process, by being present to your daily life. Focus on the journey and moving forward in your life and allow the outcome to evolve accordingly.

Blaze your own specific trail.

Take Action

Experiential learning is the fastest way to learn anything. You can read all the books in the world, but if you don't actually take action, all that knowledge just remains in your head. You might think you know something, but until you actually do it, it's hypothetical. For example, many of the world's greatest inventors lacked any scientific training and perfected their ideas through trial and error.

Experience links theory to practice, assists in memory retention, leads to development of skills, and improves your confidence around that activity. Keep experimenting. Keep applying your knowledge, wisdom, and understanding to each action. Everything you do is research that moves you closer to your vision.

For a long time, I had a dream in my heart to be an entrepreneur and I kept placing that dream in the distant future, with statements that started with "One day . . . " or "When I have enough . . . " But after a while, I could no longer ignore or wait for the right conditions to start. I didn't have a lot of money, but I had a vision, felt a passion, and was willing to go for it.

Early in my career, a mentor said to me, "You don't have to get it right, you just have to get it going." After that, I did some research and built my very first website by myself. It wasn't perfect, but it was enough to get me started.

Unbreakable confidence is composed of many things, but at its core, it's the willingness to throw yourself into the fire. Many people think they need all kinds of experience and knowledge to start, but there is no line to step over, where some expert says, "You're ready!" When people wait for the "right" moment to take a risk, they end up stalling out. Don't wait for the perfect conditions to get started; convince yourself that now is the best time to take a leap. Instead of waiting for the "right" conditions, create the conditions.

Remember, you don't have to build your confidence before you do something. Confidence is built after you do something. Confidence is already inside you and increases as a result of taking action.

Take Note of How Often You Say:

* "When I have . . . , then I'll . . . "
* "I'll do it later."
* "Not now."
* "I can't because I have bills to pay."
* "I'm not ready."
* "I need more experience."

These are just thoughts that are stopping you from taking action. Even the smallest of actions, taken each day, can build confidence and forward momentum toward your vision.

The Discipline to Act

Your daily habits cultivate your vision. Break your vision down into small action steps. Seeds that you plant today will flower tomorrow. If you are continuously sowing seeds, you can eventually reap what you sow.

Everyone wants freedom, and the way to get there is through discipline. Being able to do the hard things that will make you happy in the long run (even when you don't feel like it) is what sets winners apart. It requires the ability to say "no" to the temptation of comfort and familiar, unsatisfying patterns. The more discomfort you can get through, the more courageous and confident you become. You recognize that you can handle it.

If you can take action in service of your vision, even when you don't feel like it, you will get what you want. Even the projects you feel the most passionate about will require discipline to reach fruition. Success and confidence are not something you have every once in a while, but rather what you must repeat daily.

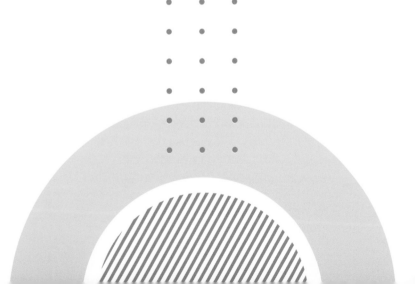

What are some specific actions you could take to move you closer to your vision? For example . . .

* Signing up for a race you've always wanted to do.

* Volunteering or getting involved in a local charity.

* Telling someone you love them.

* Setting a boundary that will create more freedom.

* Looking for a new job that you are passionate about.

* Starting the business you've been dreaming of starting.

These types of sustained changes in your life will create friction. Your mind will resist and be inclined to lean toward comfort, safety, and familiarity. Cultivating discipline in the face of this resistance is a constant internal conversation that looks like this:

* Not ready to post an inspirational quote on Instagram? Share it.

* Not ready to write your first article? Write it.

* Not ready to start that website? Start it.

* Not ready to speak up and share your ideas in a meeting? Speak it.

* Don't "feel" like going to the gym? Go anyway.

* Don't "feel" like having the uncomfortable conversation of asking for a raise? Ask anyway.

* Don't "feel" like eating something healthy? Make the healthy choice anyway.

When I was in full challenge mode in my younger days, I went to yoga class regularly. My teacher said, "Discipline leads to freedom," and that stuck with me because it was exactly what I needed to hear. In my quest for freedom, I didn't want any rules. I used to think of discipline as harsh and rigid. Discipline seemed limiting, but I quickly realized the opposite is true. Show up when you don't want to, and you start to see results.

Discipline is the real work behind the scenes that creates these results; discipline is all the practice, preparation, and everything else that people don't see. It's when you don't get the pat on the back. It's the hard work, sacrifice, failure, risk, rejection, persistence, and confidence in your ability to get back up and keep moving in spite of whatever arises. Life is uncomfortable whichever way you look at it, so you might as well get uncomfortable in pursuing your potential because the rewards can be huge.

When Lady Gaga won the Best Original Song Academy Award for "Shallow," she gave an emotional acceptance speech to mark the moment. She said, "If you are at home, and you're sitting on your couch and you're watching this right now, all I have to say is that this is hard work. I've worked hard for a long time, and it's not about, you know . . . it's not about winning. But what it's about is not giving up. If you have a dream, fight for it. There's a discipline for passion. And it's not about how many times you get rejected or you fall down, or you're beaten up. It's about how many times you stand up and are brave and you keep on going."

Rarely is there a right time to do things that are hard, risky, uncomfortable, or scary. Instead of leaning into the negativity bias that tells you why you can't indulge your heart's desire, try to look for the reasons why you can and follow that spark. Trust yourself even when you don't have it all figured out.

IGNITE YOUR ACTIONS

WITH INTENTION

Having a greater sense of the purpose of your actions can help you move forward. For example, I have a friend who has written a horror novel. She's had a hard time moving forward on seeking an agent and putting it out into the world. But when I asked her what her intention was, she said, "I want readers to have an experience that I know they will enjoy." Once she said this, a light bulb went off in her head and she said, "Oh yeah, that's why I'm doing this!" She was immediately taken out of all her own fears and trepidation and was focused on creating a positive experience for others. When your actions are aligned with something larger than yourself, it becomes easier to act.

Intention is about the energy you bring to each action—it's how you are "being" and the impact your energy has on those around you. It's the reason why you are doing what you are doing and how you wish to contribute to the world.

In an interview with LinkedIn CEO Jeff Weiner, Oprah Winfrey shared that after she read *The Seat of the Soul* by Gary Zukav, she began to apply the principle of intention to her career. She said, "The number one principle that rules my life is intention." After reading Zukav's book, she had a big meeting with all her producers and said they were going to become an intentional television show. She explained to her producers that the idea behind it—the vision—was that they were going to be a force for good.

Winfrey explained that there were many times when she was pitched ideas that had plenty of interesting details but no positive intention, and she turned them down. There were other times she dismissed pitches where she could tell the producer was manufacturing an intention they didn't believe in. Winfrey said that this philosophy still drives everything she does, because "I have to be able to find for myself the thread of truth that I can hold on to, and sit in the chair, and be an authentic person."

When you create an intention, it sets the stage for your actions, and it's likely this will have a positive impact on your life. So begin by checking in on your intention. Be honest with yourself. Why did you pick up this book? Why is your vision important to you? What's underneath this vision that's motivating you? How will this vision help others?

When someone gives a gift and has a good intention, we feel it. When someone makes us a meal and they have a good intention, we taste it. Intention is something that we feel. Even when your actions are misunderstood, you can be confident on the basis of having had a good intention. If you know in your heart that your intention was good, even if something doesn't work out, you will feel positively, because you tried to do good.

CREATE YOUR INTENTION TO:

* Help others
* Make a positive impact

* Do good for the benefit of all
* Do what's best

Don't Take It Personally

The path you choose might not be what others think you should do. There can be so much pressure from family, friends, and society to live a certain way, but it's important to live according to your intention. It's impossible to gain everyone's approval. Be more concerned about what you think and feel about yourself than what others do.

When you forge a new path or begin something new, it's likely that others will be more than happy to share their beliefs and opinions about why they think it is a bad idea. People do this for two basic reasons:

1. They care about you and are projecting their fear.

2. It subtly gives rise for them to question their own choices. Because our brains are wired for safety and efficiency, it's natural for others to resist you changing.

When you speak of your vision to a friend and they express doubt, they are most probably projecting their own beliefs and limitations onto you. And guess what? You do not have to accept these limitations. You can thank them for sharing their view and share your view, or quietly know in your heart that their opinion is not your truth.

Because you are unique, you've had your own experiences and have an original perspective on the world. Your path shouldn't look like anyone else's. Your trail will differ from those around you. Stop comparing your life to those of other people and give yourself permission to rewrite whatever "rules" you've internalized. You are here to fulfill your highest vision. Nobody else has, or ever will, walk exactly in your shoes.

· · ·

· · ·

Here's a Fact

As you move in the direction of your highest vision, you will piss some people off. If you're a recovering people-pleaser like myself, this is a hard pill to swallow. I know it feels good to make other people feel happy, but not at your own expense. Free yourself from the burden of other people's opinions and expectations and the need for their approval.

Here is a step-by-step process to help you take specific action toward your vision.

1. *Reveal* your intention.

A statement of intent is a description that inspires, energizes, and moves you in the direction of your vision by putting the focus on how others will feel a positive emotion based on you taking action.

Write your statement of intent: I want to _____
that makes others feel _____ because I love _____.

Now is the time to complete any unfinished business, such as updating your resume or completing your book project.

2. *Research* information.

Map out what information you need and make a list of the people or companies you want to connect with. For example, if you want to get a new job, you'll want to research companies and brands you love. If you want to start a new business, you'll want to gather information about what you need to do to get started and make a list of potential clients you could work with. If you want to get your book published, make a list of agents who represent writers in your genre.

Once you have this list, find people's email addresses. To do this, you can go to LinkedIn and search for people's names or search by company name. If the email is not listed there, you can do a search on rocketreach.co.

Keep track of your contact names and information by creating a spreadsheet like this one.

Company	Contact Name	Contact Email	Date of Outreach

3. *Reach* out to contacts.

Because people get so many emails, you want to make yours stand out. Write an email or cover letter that reveals your intention to work with them. Make it more about what you can give and do for them. Tell your story to connect with the reader emotionally. When you connect with the reader emotionally, you win. Reveal why you are the person to work with and what you have to offer.

When my client Alex came to me for coaching, she felt unfulfilled and dispassionate at her job as an account manager at a health insurance company. After a few of our coaching sessions, it became clear that her real passion was for food. So, she made a list of brands and companies that she loved and used in her own home. Then she went to those company websites and applied for jobs.

Since she was making a transition in her career, she believed that she was going to have to take a pay cut if she transitioned into a field in which she had "no experience," but she quickly realized this wasn't true. She used her personal experience and passion, combined with the practical skills she had developed working for an insurance company, to pitch herself.

Take a look at the cover letter she wrote (she got the job and was paid more than she was making in insurance!). In many cases, people want to work with people who are passionate! This email and cover letter method has worked many times. Formulate your story and connect it to the person or brand with which you wish to forge a relationship. Tell them why you care about them or their business and how you can contribute to their mission.

Don't get intimidated by sending an email. It's just an email! The next two pages have Alex's sample cover letter to help give you some inspiration for your outreach efforts.

4. *Repeat.*

Follow up, don't get discouraged, and be persistent. You'll get rejections, but keep going and apply consistent effort and discipline.

Hello,

My name is Alexandra Kitz, and I'm a bit of a paradox. I'm a South Carolinian, a Southern belle with an appreciation for the fast pace and quick wit of the Northeast. I love hot dogs, but I'm equally as enthusiastic about escargot. I'm a senior account manager at a health insurance brokerage firm, but my true passion is food. However, like French fries and artisanal mayonnaise, I believe two things that probably shouldn't go together can come together to create a magical result. Please keep an open mind and read further to learn how I can use my experience to promote the hell out of Sir Kensington's charming condiments. (Condiments that I use in my own home and love!)

As you will see in my resume, my experience aligns well with the demands and responsibilities of your market manager position. Professionally, I thrive on my ability to cultivate deep client relationships while also fostering a productive, fun, and engaging environment with my colleagues. The key strengths I possess for success in this position include, but are certainly not limited to, the following:

* Excellent communication, relationship building, and organizational skills

* Proven retention and sales achievements

* Ability to manage multiple competing deadlines in an efficient, calm, and reassuring manner

* Eager and quick to learn and grow—especially if the journey involves food!

* Detail oriented is putting it lightly, (When I'm not explaining how insurance works, I'm wrestling with carriers over pricing and contract negotiations.)

* Energetic and collegial team player

* Contacts throughout the East Coast in multiple food and beverage industries (hello, South Carolina!)

Please consider this: I did not enter into my current field with a strong interest in health insurance. However, with only five years in the business, I have mastered the complex intricacies, and I am regarded by my company and clients as a trusted expert. If I can learn to navigate the Affordable Care Act and sell health insurance with confidence, imagine how quickly I can become a brand ambassador for all things Sir Kensington's! Let's find out together.

I hope you will find that my business acumen, proven success in relationship management, and sharp communication skills are intriguing enough to warrant a face-to-face meeting. I am well-spoken, energetic, confident, and personable—the type of person you and your colleagues can rely on. I am excited about the opportunity to work for Sir Kensington's and hope to meet you soon.

Thank you for your time and consideration. I look forward to speaking with you.

Sincerely,
Alexandra Kitz

I AM RESPONSIBLE FOR MY ACTIONS.

I always do my best.

TAKE CARE OF YOURSELF

"An empty lantern provides no light. *Self-care* is the fuel that allows *your light* to shine brightly."

—UNKNOWN

You can't expect yourself to perform at your highest level if you don't take care of yourself and treat yourself well. It's important to care for your body, mind, and spirit to have sustainable energy to make lasting changes. When you push away from things that contribute to your physical, emotional, and spiritual well-being, you deplete your confidence. You can't expect yourself to walk through a desert without getting thirsty, and you can't expect yourself to do "hard" physical and emotional work without proper nourishment.

Taking care of yourself isn't selfish. In fact, when your cup is full, it's easier to be effective and helpful to others. There was a time when my son was a baby and I wasn't getting much sleep. This had a huge impact on my attitude; I got angry more easily, was less patient, and the quality of my thoughts and my energy were low. The way I was showing up in the world wasn't helpful to anyone. There is a direct correlation between how we treat ourselves and how we treat others. When you don't nourish yourself first, it affects everything, including your confidence.

Engaging in activities that give you energy creates an inner environment for you to thrive and manage difficulties with the ability to bounce back. And because so much of life is uncertain, one of the few things you have some agency over is how you choose to treat yourself.

This isn't about taking care of yourself "perfectly." Avoid militantly policing these activities as a form of negative reinforcement or punishment. That's not what I'm talking about. I'm talking about embracing the intention of being healthy and supportive to yourself so you can be at your best. Exercising and consuming healthy food are strong ways of taking care of your mind and body so that you can operate at your peak performance. Following is a list of activities that can boost your energy and confidence.

. . . .

Exercise

Movement in your body creates movement in your life. If you are feeling stuck metaphorically, physically move. Exercise has many benefits, such as relieving symptoms of depression, keeping your heart and bones strong, promoting blood flow and oxygen to your brain, and releasing endorphins. Endorphins are known to help produce positive feelings and reduce the perception of pain. If you're feeling tired or down, exercise can pick your energy up. The Centers for Disease Control and Prevention encourage most adults to get at least 150 minutes of moderate-intensity aerobic activity per week.

Healthy Food

Food is a big part of our everyday lives, and eating well is a key aspect of taking care of yourself. As much as you can, avoid processed foods; eat plenty of fruits, vegetables, and whole foods; and drink water. Again, this isn't about being perfect, but about treating yourself well and noticing how food affects your body, mind, and energy levels. Most of us know the basics about healthy eating, so don't overcomplicate things. Keep it simple.

Proper nutrition also affects your thoughts and emotions. When I wasn't eating well, I suffered from anxiety and depression. I know from my own experience that an important part of my healing was learning to eat well and listen to my body. It took me years to adjust my diet, but I'm so grateful I did. I now have occasional sweets, but I don't eat them often because I don't like the way they make me feel.

When I cleaned up my diet, my energy and happiness increased. I also created a more peaceful relationship with food. I began to think about food with regard to energy instead of using it as a source of emotional pleasure and to avoid emotional pain. The first step is noticing how you feel after you eat something. Does the feeling align with how you want to feel? If not, you can make adjustments.

Yoga

The word yoga, from the Sanskrit word yuj, means to "yoke" or "bind;" it is often interpreted as "union," or a method of discipline to reconnect to yourself. It's about gaining inner awareness, not about making your butt look better (although that might be a secondary benefit). Yoga has been around for more than 5,000 years for a reason: it has many healing effects on the body, mind, and spirit. Yoga practice encourages you to connect with your breath and allows vital energy to flow.

There are many types of yoga, so if you've tried one and don't like it, I encourage you to try another. Iyengar has been my favorite way to manage stress. It has taught me to stay in situations when they get tough, instead of defaulting to my old reactions.

Acupuncture

Acupuncture is all about the harmonious balance of meridians, or pathways of energy in the human body called qi. The insertion of small needles into the skin sends new blood to the area and helps promote healing. Note: The needles don't hurt. I used to be scared of them!

Journaling

The practice of putting your uncensored thoughts on paper helps give you clarity. Journaling also releases you from the thoughts swirling around in your head and creates the opportunity for you to be more aware of what you're thinking and feeling. This awareness can be a catalyst for change.

Creativity

Do things that exercise your ability to be creative—paint, draw, dance, make a collage, or whatever gets you in the flow. Being creative helps improve the process of problem solving because it allows your brain to make connections.

Music

Listening to music can ground you. You can disappear into the sounds and lyrics and feel yourself more fully in your body. Music makes us want to move, and this is always a good thing in terms of mood. Test yourself. The next time you're obsessed with a problem, circling the drain over and over in your mind, crank up your playlist and dance. See how quickly you are smiling and laughing, all thoughts released by the rhythm and beat of the music.

Financial Management

Money can be a source of stress and anxiety. Finances can be highly charged and emotional. Managing your finances is an important part of taking care of yourself. What's most important is making a commitment to the basics: budgeting, saving, and eliminating debt. Make savings a habit. Even if you save only five dollars a week, it's part of taking care of yourself. Automate as much as you can. Educate yourself around the topic.

Some people ignore their finances out of fear. If they don't look, they think they don't have to deal with it. This creates so much anxiety because money is part of your everyday life. If it's too difficult, seek professional guidance from a fiduciary or financial expert. One of my favorite books on this topic is *The Total Money Makeover* by Dave Ramsey. I have a Dave Ramsey Certified Coach and he has helped me with budgeting, investing, and financial planning. Having a money management strategy gives you more clarity and confidence.

Decluttering

When your space is cluttered and chaotic, your clarity, confidence, and performance weaken. Decluttering promotes a sense of calm and positivity. Organize your closet or desk. Get rid of things in your space that don't lift you up. Make your environment a place where you can feel good.

Meditation

We touched on meditation in chapter 4 (page 61), but I'll say it again: meditation is an important part of self-care. Meditation creates awareness, and awareness is power. If you've practiced meditation before and felt like your mind was too busy, you are completely normal. Don't get discouraged. You can't expect yourself to do something once and be an expert. Keep practicing. Start with five minutes. Practicing meditation helps you become a better manager of your thoughts. It is medicine for my mind.

Volunteer Work

Doing something for others and giving back to the community increases a sense of purpose and well-being. Volunteering gives you confidence, because you know you have the power to help others. It also provides perspective on your problems. Perhaps you volunteer for a food bank, and it increases your awareness of how much you have. Find a "problem" you are passionate about and volunteer your time or money.

Practice Kindness Toward Others

Whenever I am feeling down, the quickest way to lift myself up is by doing something kind for someone else. I found a credit card in a grocery store parking lot and picked it up and Facebook and messaged her asking if she had lost a credit card. When we met up and I returned her card, she tried to give me a $50 bill, but I refused it. She thought I had made her day, but in reality, she had made mine. It is so uplifting to help others. I felt so wonderful helping her.

After a positive experience, your brain makes new connections and pathways toward feeling good. According to research from Emory University, when you are kind to another person, your brain's pleasure and reward centers light up as if you were the recipient of the good deed—not the giver. This phenomenon has earned the nickname "helper's high" among psychologists who study generosity, and some researchers theorize that the sensation is also due to a release of endorphins, those feel-good chemicals associated with runner's high.

These studies show that what matters most isn't how much knowledge you accumulate, what you did on Friday night, or how many followers you have on Instagram. What matters most is how you treat others.

Engage in acts of kindness and you will see your authentic confidence naturally increase. Any act of kindness counts: a smile, helping someone cross the street, contributing to a charity, picking up trash, opening the door for someone, and so much more.

To help you focus on a kindness practice, keep a kindness journal. Write down the acts of kindness you perform each day. Know the good you did, no matter the size of the act. Acknowledge the fact that you are beneficial to others. This allows you to feel happier and make a positive impact in the world. Make kindness deposits everywhere you go!

Here are some other reasons to be kind.

* The positive effect of kindness on the immune system and the increased production of serotonin in the brain have been proven in research studies. A naturally occurring substance in the body, serotonin makes us feel more comfortable, peaceful, and even blissful.

* Humans often mimic behavior they see, and that includes generosity, which explains why some of these stories of small acts of kindness become bigger news: even people who simply hear about a giving chain are often inspired to give, starting a succession of positivity all their own. A person who has just received any bit of kindness is elevated, happy, and grateful, making them likely to help someone else, according to a 2007 study from Harvard University.

Unconditional Friendship with Yourself

Thoughts are energy, so take off the boxing gloves and stop beating yourself up. Stop attacking, criticizing yourself, and putting yourself down. This drains your energy.

Being gentle with yourself creates confidence. Being hard on yourself doesn't help you or anyone else. The Sanskrit word *maitri* can be roughly translated as "an unconditional friendship towards oneself." Unconditional friendship means you love yourself no matter what.

Sometimes we think we need validation from the outside. We wait for someone to say, "Hey, you did a great job," or we're

> "The root of true *confidence* grows from our ability to be in unconditional *friendship with ourselves.*"
>
> —PEMA CHÖDRÖN

afraid to do something new because we haven't done it before. I hear many people disqualify themselves before they even try. Develop positive self-talk where you validate yourself and your efforts. Take the risk, then affirm yourself: "Great job!" Pat yourself on the back. Treat yourself with the same love, kindness, and support that you'd offer your closest friends or a child.

This doesn't mean that you should view yourself through rose-colored glasses, but rather that you accept your mistakes, shortcomings, and missteps with kindness. When a child is learning to walk and falls down, you don't criticize them. You keep encouraging them. Maintain a zero-tolerance rule for unkind thoughts and self-criticism. Applying this one principle will, at the very least, increase your happiness. Ultimately, you want to befriend yourself as you navigate the ups and downs of life, not just by loving yourself when things are good, but also by showing compassion for yourself when things are hard. This is necessary to create unconditional confidence.

Here is an invitation to unconditional friendship with yourself . . .

 * Can you love yourself when you make a mistake?

 * Can you love yourself when things don't go your way?

 * Can you be kind even when you don't want to?

 * What can you do each day to create pure positive energy?

You wouldn't say some of the things you say to yourself to a friend. So, raise the standards for friendship with yourself. Practice non-harmful thinking.

Align Your Values

When you connect your goals to your personal values, it's easier to follow through with behavioral changes that will help you cultivate your vision.

If you're ready to step into the most confident version of yourself, you need to understand what is really important to you. Most people are living unconscious to their value system, or have values that were passed down to them rather than consciously chosen. Values are a set of standards based on what's most important to you. When you uncover and understand what your true values are, it's easier to make confident decisions.

Values help you direct your attention and live in alignment with what you really care about. Making deliberate choices guided by your values allows you to live a life you intentionally designed. These decisions create your destiny. The core values you choose are there to inspire you. For example, values could include learning, creativity, adventure, openness, or inner harmony.

Growth is one of my top values. When I am growing and learning, I have energy. Learning feeds my soul. Because of this, I make time to learn every day. I do this through audiobooks, reading, listening to podcasts, attending classes or retreats, asking questions, and having conversations with people who inspire me. I make time to learn every day.

After having a conversation with a friend about how much I love podcasts, because I learn something new every time I listen, she replied, "You could have your own podcast!" In response to this "aha!" moment, I decided to create a podcast where I get to bring this value to life.

Your values may or may not align with traditional values you've been taught growing up (and that's okay!), so keep an open mind. Ask yourself tough questions to get rewarding results that last. Listen to your intuition when it says, "This makes me so happy!" and then try and ascribe a value to whatever it is that brings you the most joy. Once you know what your values are, it will be easier to lead your life with intention. You'll be able to make bold decisions confidently about the changes you want to make and the opportunities you want to pursue.

CHOOSE YOUR CORE VALUES

Being values-driven helps you stay connected to what's truly important to you and to determine whether or not something is in alignment. As you grow and change, your values might grow and change. Be willing to update your values often.

1. Abundance
2. Acceptance
3. Adaptability
4. Adventure
5. Ambition
6. Appreciation
7. Autonomy
8. Balance
9. Beauty
10. Boldness
11. Bravery
12. Calmness
13. Caring
14. Clarity
15. Confidence
16. Connection
17. Contribution
18. Courage
19. Creativity
20. Curiosity
21. Daring
22. Decisiveness
23. Determination
24. Diligence
25. Discipline
26. Discovery
27. Empathy
28. Encouragement
29. Energy
30. Enjoyment
31. Enlightenment
32. Entrepreneurial
33. Expression
34. Faith
35. Family
36. Flexibility
37. Focus
38. Friendship
39. Fun
40. Generosity
41. Gratitude
42. Growth
43. Happiness
44. Harmony
45. Health
46. Helpfulness
47. Honesty
48. Hope

49. Humility	71. Openness	93. Sharing
50. Humor	72. Opportunity	94. Simplicity
51. Imagination	73. Optimism	95. Solidarity
52. Inspiration	74. Organization	96. Spirituality
53. Integrity	75. Originality	97. Stillness
54. Intuition	76. Passion	98. Strength
55. Joy	77. Patience	99. Success
56. Justice	78. Peace	100. Teamwork
57. Kindness	79. Persistence	101. Tranquility
58. Knowledge	80. Playfulness	102. Transcendence
59. Leadership	81. Pleasure	103. Trust
60. Learning	82. Power	104. Truth
61. Love	83. Privacy	105. Understanding
62. Loyalty	84. Purpose	106. Uniqueness
63. Magic	85. Reflection	107. Unity
64. Mastery	86. Reliability	108. Variety
65. Mindfulness	87. Resilience	109. Vision
66. Modesty	88. Resourcefulness	110. Willingness
67. Motivation	89. Respectful	111. Wisdom
68. Newness	90. Responsibility	112. Wonder
69. Nourishment	91. Security	113. Zealous
70. Nurturing	92. Sensitivity	

Choose the top five values from this list that inspire you:

1._____   3._____   5._____

2._____   4._____

INTEGRATE YOUR CORE VALUES

Think about the top five values that you chose from the previous page. As you make choices going forward, if something intuitively doesn't "feel right," check in with these values to make sure you're living an authentic life.

Ask yourself the following questions for each of your core values.

★ What does honoring this value look like?

★ What does this value guide me to do?

★ How do I incorporate this value more in my day-to-day life?

★ Does your job align with what you care about?

★ Do your values align with your relationships?

When you design your life according to your values, you set yourself up to experience true confidence.

I ENGAGE IN ACTIVITIES THAT FILL ME UP.

I TAKE GOOD care of myself.

"Always do your *BEST*. What you plant now, you will *HARVEST* later."

—OG MANDINO

Building confidence isn't an overnight or quick-fix process. It's a journey of discovery and rediscovery, over and over again, as you move forward and grow as a person. Becoming confident isn't about becoming someone new, but uncovering who you really are at your core.

Every day presents an opportunity, and you can choose to reinforce the limitations already in your head, or learn how to connect with yourself and get acquainted with the indestructible essence of your being. Just as the surface of an ocean has turbulent waves, there is calm beneath the surface. The turbulent waters represents your egoic thoughts. But underneath, there's a calm confidence that is the essence of who you are.

It takes courage to step out of the habitual patterns, because when you do, you enter an open space of uncertainty. But in this space is the opportunity for you to be aware of your authentic power. In this space, you must let go of your ego identity and how you once perceived yourself. You must trust in the basic goodness that's already within you. Each choice you make to follow the spark of trusting your own goodness lights the path forward and allows you to make a positive impact on the world.

Growth requires patience, courage, understanding, resilience, softness, and strength. Confidence is about expanding your capacity to feel into the human experience, which includes all kinds of joy and sorrow, knowing that through it all you are unbreakable!

Budding Confidence

Throughout this book, I shared strategies for identifying the ego thoughts that hold you back and how to lean into the confidence seed inside you. You have to nurture that seed so it continues to grow. From the moment you wake up in the morning, connect to the experience of being confident. Engage in practices that nurture growth on a daily basis.

Is the water for your seed meditation? Exercise? Yoga? Journaling? Do you have negative friends who are weeds, crowding out your light? Are you giving your seed the proper nutrients of healthy food and sleep?

You can be a work in progress and still be confident. You will go through different seasons—sometimes storms will appear, but they will pass. There will be seasons where you need to apply more effort and seasons where you enjoy the fruits of your labor.

This process of growing confidence is made up of very small changes over time. As I said earlier, there is no "arrival" at some destination, only small daily steps. I still don't jump up in the morning all peaches and roses, but I wake up knowing that there's opportunity in each day to grow, and that the harvest will come.

Be aware of your thoughts and stay in action. If you are having trouble getting into action, start with the smalles step and only push yourself to complete that tiny task. If you don't feel like working out, put on your workout clothes. Then, if you're still feeling empowered, do the next lowest barrier of entry action. Perhaps prior to working out, you just go for a walk. Once you've shown yourself that this big action is actually only comprised of several small steps, you'll be more apt to take big action.

This applies to all things such as writing, cleaning, and so on. Look for the act that has the least resistance but still moves you in the direction of the higher action. You will reap what you sow.

Achieving my dream didn't happen overnight. Coaching was my side-hustle for many years before I was able to take a bigger leap and create my own company. I took uncomfortable steps and risks that fostered new relationships that support me personally and professionally. I tuned into my body over and over again, and learned to take better care of myself.

I still stumble and fall down. I still get confronted with challenges and obstacles. I don't have it all figured out, but one thing I know is that if you don't let the ego's voice in your head stop you, you will become unstoppable. The world needs the bolder you. And when you shine your light, you give others the permission to shine too!

Make small shifts in how you view yourself, spend your mornings talking to yourself; be conscious of what you read, view, and listen to. Repeated daily, these actions can make a profound impact in your life.

Choose to Be Confident

Life's challenges are inevitable. A confident person doesn't have it all together, or all figured out, but they trust themselves and life, even when things get rocky. Confident people have struggles, weaknesses, and fear. But these people just identify more with their strengths than with their weaknesses, focus on the good, direct their imagination toward things going well, and know that positive living is a matter of choice, not circumstance.

Those who have to cultivate confidence take risks, face their fears, and step out of their comfort zones over and over again. Growth is uncomfortable, and sometimes painful, but this is when you learn the most. Things will fall apart, and new things will come together. No journey happens in a straight line. The rewards might not come right away, but with persistence, determination, patience, and effort, growth will occur.

There is a story about a little boy who was playing outdoors, and he found a caterpillar. He watched the caterpillar climb up the tree and act strangely. His mother explained that the caterpillar was forming a cocoon to become a butterfly. The little boy watched it every day, waiting for the butterfly to emerge. And one day a small hole appeared in the cocoon and the butterfly struggled to come out.

At first, the boy was really excited. As time passed, he became concerned because the butterfly was trying so hard to get out and he feared it wouldn't break free. Frightened and worried, he ran to get scissors. He then snipped the cocoon to make the hole bigger, and the butterfly quickly emerged.

But when the butterfly came out, the boy was surprised to see that the body was swollen and the wings were shriveled. He continued to watch the butterfly, expecting that at any moment the wings would dry out and expand so the butterfly could fly away.

But that didn't happen.

Instead, the butterfly spent the rest of its life crawling around with a swollen body and shriveled wings. It was never able to fly. The boy tried to figure out what had gone wrong. He went to a local college to see a scientist and he learned that the butterfly was supposed to struggle to get out of the cocoon. As the butterfly pushed its way through the tiny opening of the cocoon, it flushed the fluid out of its body and into its wings. Without the struggle, the butterfly would be unable to fly.

As you go through life, keep in mind that sometimes struggling is an important part of growth. It allows you to develop the strength to fly. Embrace struggle as part of the journey to build emotional strength and confidence.

Stand rooted in unbreakable confidence. Make a choice to live a confident life.

. . . .

Nurture The Seed

There is valuable support out there to help you nurture your seed of confidence. Sometimes strengths can come so naturally to you that you might not even recognize your innate talents.

Bre came to me for coaching because she was feeling stuck and unfulfilled in her career. Her educational background was in health sciences and she was working at a desk job in finance. I asked Bre to list the things she was passionate about. This was when, for the first time, Bre talked about her love for and interest in makeup. All of her friends came to her for makeup advice, and she was often buying new products and experimenting with different colors and looks in her free time.

However, she was doubtful she could make enough money doing this as a profession. She believed a career as a makeup artist was shallow and thought she would have to stand at a makeup counter in a department store all day. She felt it was superficial to apply makeup on people who wanted to look "pretty" and believed that even a "brain-dead duck" could do makeup. These beliefs prevented her from using her innate talent as a makeup artist. I began asking her questions about how people behave when they *feel* pretty. She responded that feeling beautiful encourages people to feel happier, be more loving, and express kindness towards others. I asked, "Does that make a positive impact on the world?" She grinned and said, "Yes!" When she made the connection that makeup has a positive impact on making others feel good in their lives, it completely shifted her view.

Things changed course after that. Bre posted a photo of her makeup artistry on her Facebook page and a friend asked if she would be interested in working at a photo shoot. She took the job and it was a huge success. The photos looked great and helped Bre get her first real gig. Within five weeks of letting go of her job in finance, she earned $1,500 from a one-day shoot. One thing led to another, and Bre was soon working for renowned makeup companies. Bre had always wanted a billboard of her own work to be featured in Times Square, and in 2016 her dream came true. Her business continues to grow and she has worked for so many people all around the world. She is able to comfortably support herself, and she volunteers doing makeup for cancer patients. Her work is fulfilling, she is respected by others, and she gets to travel all over the world.

Bre had never even considered that her love for makeup would change her career path. With the guidance of objective and trained eyes on her situation (a coach), she was able to recognize her passion and see its value in the world as well as to her own happiness.

Have Faith in Your Potential

In the past twenty-five years, neuroscience has discovered the brain's ability to make new connections. This is called neuroplasticity. Neuroplasticity is the change in neural pathways and synapses that occurs due to certain factors, like behavior, environment, or neural processes. During such changes, the brain engages in making new connections by transmitting an electrical or a chemical signal to another neuron, deleting the neural connections that are no longer necessary or useful, and strengthening the new ones that are.

In other words, your brain has the ability to change. And because of neuroplasticity, the act of paying attention to something creates chemical and physical changes in the brain.

By deliberately focusing your point of attention, new feelings occur. When you let go of old ways of being consumed by thinking and focus your attention on being a confident person, it creates new neural pathways. The emotions you choose to focus on are the ones you feel. Is it as simple as letting go of old thoughts and stories? Inhabiting new emotions, you want to experience? To some extent, yes. But just because it's easy to explain this process doesn't make it easy to embody. Have faith in your ability even when there are storms.

Cultivate Your Confident Identity

Growing up, I was a shy kid. I can remember hiding behind my mom's leg whenever we were out in public and someone wanted to talk to me. As a teen, I had my friends speak up for me in restaurants and stores. Many years later, in my adult life, my best friend—who used to speak up for me—attended one of my live talks. She reminded me how shy I used to be and said how proud she was that I could now speak in front of large groups.

For many years I believed that being shy was who I was. But not anymore. I no longer identify with being shy. I sometimes feel nervous prior to speaking to groups, but I remind myself that this is the voice of my ego, and I'll be okay if I lead from my heart.

Awareness is like a friend that never lets you down. Awareness is a guide that is always there to support you, even when it notices you are out of alignment. I still have a voice in my head, but it doesn't consume me anymore. Of course, every once in a while I get lured into the false narrative, but I don't stay in the story because I recognize it as a story.

Feeling confident might feel strange or different at first, but that's mostly because you're familiar with not feeling confident. When something is strange and unfamiliar to us, it tends to feel uncomfortable, so your brain can think the feeling is fake. Have you ever gotten a new computer and at first it feels a bit confusing and you miss your old computer, but over time you get so used to the new device that you can't imagine going back to the old one?

Continue to update your belief operating system to support your confident identity. Develop faith in yourself and your ability by doing things that are challenging, that test your growth edge, that show you are more capable than you think. Each small victory builds your confidence, and over time, things that used to intimidate you can become easy. Start small and simply imagine yourself taking action despite your fears and uncertainty. If you do this regularly, you will begin to see yourself in a new way. With repetition, this belief becomes your confident identity. And because behavior follows identity, you will continue to reinforce your confident self.

Familiarize yourself with feeling confident. Make your confidence seed bigger and brighter—make your bold voice loud. Grow your confidence seed by focusing your attention on what it feels like to be irrevocably yourself: How would you think? How would you act? Answer these questions from the heart: Are you making decisions guided by fear of the future or an unbreakable faith in yourself? When you make choices from a place of confidence, you create a new destiny.

Listen to the voice that says, you are unbreakable!

"Little by little, a little becomes *A LOT*."

—TANZANIAN PROVERB

SHINE LIGHT ON YOUR CONFIDENCE SEED

If you want to create a new result, you must start with recognizing your habitual thoughts and repetitive thought patterns. The ego voice doesn't go away, but you can choose to make your confidence seed bigger, louder, and brighter.

Go back to the beginning and look at your ego story.

For example:

* I'm stuck.

* I don't have enough time to build the business of my dreams.

Now write your new story.

For example:

* I am making progress.

* I have an abundance of time.

* I have lots of energy.

* I can build the business of my dreams.

* I am manifesting my desires now.

What are your confident thoughts and story?

_____

How do those thoughts and story make you feel?

_____

If you felt confident, what actions would you take?

_____

Take action! It is through action that your confidence will continue to grow.

_____

I AM UNBREAKABLE!

I AM confident.

BOLD MANTRAS

I AM ENOUGH JUST AS I AM.

FAILURE IS A STEPPING-STONE TO SUCCESS.

IT IS SAFE FOR ME TO GROW.

I CAN CHANGE MY BELIEFS.

I PAY ATTENTION TO INTUITIVE NUDGES.

I TRUST MYSELF.

OBSTACLES ARE AN OPPORTUNITY TO GROW.

ADVERSITY GIVES ME STRENGTH.

I CREATE MY REALITY.

I AM RESPONSIBLE FOR MY ACTIONS.

I ALWAYS DO MY BEST.

I ENGAGE IN ACTIVITIES THAT FILL ME UP.

I TAKE GOOD CARE OF MYSELF.

I AM CONFIDENT.

Resources

Covey, Stephen R. *The 7 Habits of Highly Effective People.* Franklin Covey, 1998.

Chödrön, Pema. *Unconditional Confidence: Instructions for Meeting Any Experience with Trust and Courage– Unabridged.* Rec. January 1, 2010. Audio CD. 978-1591797463.

Chödrön, Pema. *When Things Fall Apart: Heart Advice for Difficult Times.* United States: Shambhala Publications, Incorporated, 2005.

Dyer, Dr Wayne W. *Everyday Wisdom for Success.* Hay House UK Ltd, 2007.

Lindley, Siri. *Surfacing: From the depths of self-doubt to winning big & living fearlessly.* Boulder, CO: Velo Press, 2016.

Pillay, Srinivasan S. M. D. *Your Brain and Business: the Neuroscience of Great Leaders.* Financial Times Pren Hall, 2014.

Robbins, Anthony. *Awaken the Giant Within: How to Take Immediate Control of Your Mental, Emotional, Physical & Financial Destiny!* Simon & Schuster Paperbacks, 2013.

Rogin, Ellen, and Lisa Kueng. *Picture Your Prosperity: Smart Money Moves to Turn Your Vision into Reality.* Portfolio / Penguin, 2015.

Schmalbruch, Sarah. "Here's The Trick Olympic Athletes Use To Achieve Their Goals." *Business Insider,* Business Insider, 28 Jan. 2015, www.businessinsider.com/olympic-athletes-and-power-of-visualization-2015-1.

Tejaniya, Ashin. *Awareness Alone is Not Enough: Q & A with Ashin Tejaniya.* Petaling Jaya: Kong Meng San Phor Kark See Monastery, 2013.

Tolle, Eckhart. *A New Earth: Awakening to Your Life's Purpose.* Penguin Books, 2018.

Zukav, G., Winfrey, O., & Angelou, M. *The Seat of the Soul: An Inspiring Vision of Humanity's Spiritual Destiny.* London: Ebury Digital, 2012.

INDEX

A

anxiety
  ego and, 21
  finance and, 116–117
  food and, 114–115
  labeling, 71
  meditation and, 61
  processing, 35
  visualization and, 85

B

beliefs
  confidence and, 52
  creation of, 46
  definition of, 45
  ego and, 48
  examination of, 47–51
  exercise, 54
  expanding beliefs, 53
  interpretation of reality
    and, 46
  learned beliefs, 48
  limiting beliefs, 48, 53
  meaning and, 46
  opinion as, 51
  power of perception,
    50–51
  supporting evidence for,
    49–50
brain
  creativity and, 116
  exercise and, 114
  fear and, 31
  kindness and, 118–119
  language and, 26
  mantras and, 9
  meditation and, 61–62

mind compared to, 12
negativity bias, 14–15,
  16
neuroplasticity, 135
reticular activating
  system (RAS),
  49, 50
survival instinct and, 14
visualization and, 84–85

C

confidence
  action and, 98–99
  awareness and, 136
  beliefs and, 45
  clutter and, 117
  cultivation of, 136–137
  definition of, 25, 52
  discipline and, 100
  emotions and, 67, 74
  exercises, 80, 138
  experiential learning
    and, 98–99
  failure and, 33
  fear and, 31, 32–35
  financial planning and,
    117
  intuition and, 57
  journey toward, 129,
    130–131
  kindness and, 117, 118
  mantras, 140
  misconceptions of, 25,
    32, 52
  neuroplasticity and, 135
  nurturing, 133–134
  resourcefulness and, 74

self-compassion and,
  120, 121
self-perception and,
  16–17
source of, 52
struggle and, 132–133
values and, 122
vision and, 97
visualization and, 86, 92
volunteer work and, 117,
  118
Wonder Woman Power
  Pose, 91

E

ego
  awareness of, 18, 28
  beliefs and, 48
  confidence and, 138
  definition of, 18
  facets of, 19–21
  intuition and, 57–58
  perception and, 48
emotions
  adversity and, 76–77, 78
  anxiety, 71
  confidence and, 67, 74
  confronting, 68–69
  default emotion, 74–75
  doubt, 70
  emotional engine,
    78–79
  emotional fitness, 67,
    73–75
  emotional intelligence,
    67, 68
  exercises, 54, 80

frustration, 71
"home base," 74–75
impatience, 71
labeling, 70–72
"negative" emotions,
    68–69
optimism, 73
perfectionism, 72
power of, 74
resistance, 70–71
sadness, 72
shame, 70
exercises
  beliefs, 53
  confidence, 80, 138
  ego, 28
  fear, 42
  intuition, 64
  painful emotions, 54
  values, 124–125, 126
  vision, 107–110
  visualization, 94

F

fear
  acknowledging, 36–39
  common fears, 37
  confidence and, 31,
      32–35
  desire and, 39
  discomfort and, 36–37
  energy of, 38
  failure and, 33
  familiarity and, 34–35
  focus and, 40
  grounding exercises, 38
  mapping exercise, 42
  normalizing, 38
  purpose of, 31

I

intuition
  belief in, 58–59
  ego and, 57–58
  exercise, 64
  meditation and, 60

as multisensory
    perception, 57
  practice with, 63
  purpose pauses, 60
  recognizing, 60
  self-care and, 60
  stimuli and, 60

M

meditation
  antidepressants
      compared to,
      61–62
  as brain training, 62
  distracting thoughts
      and, 61
  intuition and, 60
  mindfulness and, 61–62
  practicing, 62
  researching, 62
  self-care and, 117

S

self-care
  acupuncture, 115
  creative activities, 116
  decluttering, 117
  embracing, 114
  exercise, 114
  exercises, 124–125, 126
  financial management,
      116–117
  foods, 114–115
  journaling, 116
  kindness as, 118–119
  meditation, 117
  music, 116
  necessity of, 113
  self-validation as,
      120–121
  values and, 122–123,
      124–125
  volunteer work, 117
  yoga, 115

V

vision
  action toward, 98–99,
      101
  confidence and, 97
  definition of, 97
  discipline and, 100, 102
  exercise, 107–110
  experiential learning
      and, 98–99
  external resistance to,
      105–106
  individuality and,
      105–106
  intention and, 103–104
  projected limitations on,
      105–106
  values and, 122–123
visualization
  athletics and, 84–85, 86,
      89–90
  brain and, 84–85
  career and, 90–92
  confidence and, 92
  detours and, 89–92
  exercise, 94
  music and, 87–88
  obstacles, 92
  power of, 83
  Wonder Woman Power
      Pose, 91
voice in your head
  awareness of, 22–23
  ego as, 18, 19–21
  exercise, 28
  interrupting, 24
  language and, 25, 26–27
  mind compared to
      brain, 13
  negative thoughts,
      11–12, 14–15
  negativity bias, 14–15
  observing, 23, 25
  self-perception, 16–17

ABOUT THE AUTHOR

Anna Goldstein is an NYU-Certified Life & Business Coach and Host of the *Profit with Purpose Podcast*. With her shoot-from-the-hip style and keen gift for zooming straight to the heart of any issue, Anna has made her name helping clients figure out what they truly want, and to *go get it already!* For the past decade, she has been coaching professionals including Broadway actors, executives, entrepreneurs, and many more. Anna has been featured in Oprah.com, *The New York Observer*, *Time Out New York*, *SHAPE Magazine*, and *Marie Claire* and has been a guest speaker on Sirius Radio and *Martha Stewart Living*. Learn more at annagoldstein.com and connect with her on social media with the #beboldbook hashtag.